CATHOLIC TRUTHS
FOR OUR CHILDREN

CATHOLIC TRUTHS FOR OUR CHILDREN

GUIDELINES FOR PARENTS

Patti Maguire Armstrong

Preface by Steve Wood

To my husband, Mark,
who has joined me in my spiritual journey
to discover and partake in God's gift
of the Roman Catholic Church.

Nihil Obstat:	William B. Smith, S.T.D., Censor Librorum
Imprimatur:	✠ Robert A. Brucato, Vicar General Archdiocese of New York January 4, 2006

The *Nihil Obstat* and *Imprimatur* are official declarations that a book or pamphlet is free of doctrinal or moral error. No implication is contained therein that those who have granted the Nihil Obstat and Imprimatur agree with the contents, opinions, or statements expressed.

Grateful acknowledgement is made to the publishers for permission to use quotations from the following sources: Anthony Alexander, *College Apologetics*, and Anne Carroll, *Christ the King: Lord of History* (TAN Books); Jim Burnham and Fr. Frank Chacon, *Beginning Apologetics I* (San Juan Catholic Seminars); Brian Clowes: *Call to Action or Call to Apostasy?* (Human Life International); Fr. Robert Fox, *Covenant with Jesus* (Fatima Family Apostolate); James Cardinal Gibbons, *Faith of Our Fathers* (TAN Books); Karl Keating, *The Usual Suspects* and *Catholicism and Fundamentalism* (Ignatius Press); Patrick Madrid, *Surprised by Truth* (Basilica Press); Msgr. M. Francis Mannion, "Pastoral Answers," and Russell Shaw, "Why the Pope Rules" (*Our Sunday Visitor*); and Edward Sri, "Is Mary's Queenship Biblical?" (*This Rock*).

Scepter Publishers, Inc., P.O. Box 211, New York, NY 10018
www.scepterpublishers.org

ISBN 1-59417-041-X
ISBN 978-1-59417-041-6
PRINTED IN THE UNITED STATES OF AMERICA

CONTENTS

PREFACE

By Steve Wood

We are living in a time of crisis—a crisis of faith. By the time our Catholic youths leave adolescence and enter the world of work and family responsibility as adults, many have stopped going to Church. This exodus reflects nothing less than a rejection of the faith of their parents and contains the seeds of future calamity and unhappiness for everyone.

Why does this happen?

When God instituted his covenant with Abraham, He made it everlasting, binding upon all the descendants of that patriarch of many nations. What was the main role of Abraham in fulfilling this covenant? —"For I have chosen him, that he may charge his children and his household after him to keep the way of the Lord by doing righteousness and justice; so that the Lord may bring to Abraham what he has promised him" (Gen 18:19). Abraham is here being given the duty of educating his descendants in faith. Catechesis is teaching, the passing on to the next generation of a holy trust. You might say that catechesis is the glue that holds the covenant together. When that glue is missing, or too thin, or badly mixed to start with, you've got a problem. The covenant will not be maintained, and the faith of the next generation is permanently weakened.

This failure in catechesis is at the center of the crisis among Catholic youths. Teaching the Faith to your children is vital for the maintenance of the covenant, and it is a sacred obligation for all parents. There is no question here of simply letting others do the job. You must take charge and assume the responsibility. As the psalmist says, "He established a testimony

---

Steve Wood is founder of Family Life Center International, a worldwide apostolate dedicated to strengthening Christian families and spreading the truth of Catholicism. A popular television and radio host, noted author, and leader of the St. Joseph's Covenant Keepers men's movement, Steve is also a happily married father of eight children. He resides in Port Charlotte, Florida.

in Jacob, and appointed a law in Israel, which he commanded our fathers to teach to their children; that the next generation might know them . . . so that they should set their hope in God, and not forget the works of God, but keep his commandments" (Ps 78:5–7).

Today's secular and materialist society, of course, is a direct challenge to your children's faith. Unfortunately, even within the Church, there are teachers and textbooks that seek to impart a "watered-down" or trendy version of God's Truth. You must guard your children against this. You, as a Christian parent, are the first line of defense for your children, as Pope John Paul II said:

> Family catechesis therefore precedes, accompanies and enriches all other forms of catechesis. Furthermore, in places where widespread unbelief or invasive secularism makes real religious growth practically impossible, "the Church in the home" remains the one place where children and young people can receive an authentic catechesis. Thus there cannot be too great an effort on the part of Christian parents to prepare for this ministry of being their own children's catechists and to carry it out with tireless zeal (*Catechesis in Our Time*, no. 68).

Patti Maguire Armstrong has made the transition herself from self-described "cafeteria Catholic" to a woman of deep and generous faith, a faith informing her whole being, a faith that is a bedrock for her children's faith. In this book, she shows you how to be a catechist for your children. A doctorate in theology and the patience of a saint are not required—only a firm decision on your part that your children must receive what God wants them to receive: the truth of Catholic teaching. This is what the Scriptures say: "Train up a child in the way he should go, and when he is old he will not depart from it" (Prov 22:6).

This book contains what you need to know to become knowledgeable of your Faith. I am certain that, as you learn more and more about the wonder that is our Church and the joy of Christ's gospel, you too will become eager to share it, with your children, with other adults, even with missionaries of other faiths.

INTRODUCTION

"My people perish for want of knowledge"—Hosea 4:16

I believe that the Roman Catholic Church is the same one Jesus began—the original and complete package. I believe that it alone offers us all the truth and gifts that God makes available to us. Yet, not until I began having children did I begin to care about this Church one way or the other. As my children grew, so too did my desire to raise them Catholic and learn more about the Faith I had been born into.

This book is a by-product of my own learning process. My purpose in writing it is to help parents hand down Catholic teachings to their children. I understand that for many, imparting religion means first really learning it. That was my own task more than ten years ago. My hope is that by sharing what I have learned about what makes the Roman Catholic Church unique and different from other religions will help you pass on the Faith of the Church to your children.

Previously, my husband, Mark, and I lived for years as cafeteria Catholics—picking and choosing the parts of our religion we liked. If a Catholic teaching did not sit well with our lifestyle, we ignored the teaching and kept the lifestyle. More often than I care to admit, we were not even aware of the teachings.

I now think that if we had fully understood and embraced Catholic teaching, we never would have gone so far off the path. Among our lapses, we considered Sunday Mass optional, Confession unnecessary, the Pope a kind but out-of-touch man, and artificial birth control as the only rational choice in today's world. There was frequent discord within our family, but we never connected it with our deficiency in religious faith and practices.

As our children reached school age, my inadequate understanding of Catholicism began to bother me. I wanted my children to love God and love their Catholic faith, but it became increasingly clear to me that even when I knew the how's of Catholicism I frequently drew a blank on the why's.

There are many Catholics like me as I used to be—who know the inside of a cookbook better than their own religion. Years before I passed through the Catholic school system, Catholics had learned the nuts and bolts of their faith and were prepared to defend it. This ability was known as apologetics. For some reason, apologetics went by the wayside, along with the old Baltimore Catechism.

When I graduated from high school in 1975, I entered the world, along with an entire generation of Catholics, with a very weak understanding of the Catholic faith. It should come as no surprise to anyone, then, that a large percentage of the growing fundamentalist and non-denominational congregations are former Catholics who left the Church.

Catholics unfortunately have a reputation for being unable to provide reasoned and informed explanations of the Church's teachings to critics who quote the Bible in their attacks. Just listen to the following testimony by a former anti-Catholic, Tim Staples. He might have remained anti-Catholic if it had not been for an exceptional Catholic in his life:

> During my last year in the Marines, I met Matt Dula, a Catholic who really knew his faith. . . . When I first met Matt and we started talking about religion, I assumed he would be another poor Catholic that I could help get "saved the Bible way." I was in for quite a surprise. . . . I thank God that Matt had enough knowledge of and love for his faith, to give me intelligent answers about Catholicism. If it were not for him, I would not be Catholic today. . . . Unfortunately, before meeting Matt, I had encountered many Catholics who were ignorant of their beliefs and often indifferent toward their Church. Their apathy was just another sign to me that the Catholic Church was not the true Church of Jesus Christ. (Quoted in Patrick Madrid's book *Surprised by Truth*.)

Rather than the all-too-common scenario of a Scripture-quoting adversary convincing a wishy-washy Catholic that his faith is not only in error but dangerous to his soul, this story has a different ending. Matt was well versed in Church teachings and countered every one of Tim's arguments with a more convincing one, based on the Bible—Tim's own weapon of choice.

Instead of raising children who fear or, still worse, get drawn in by anti-Catholic arguments, we can teach them to know, love, and defend their Faith. The result could be, like Tim Staples's story, the conversion of a soul seeking the fullness of truth through the Catholic Church. But what is more important, we want our children to hold fast to their own religious upbringing. That means we have to *give* them one.

During this era of ecumenism among Christian churches, it is especially important for us Catholics to know our Faith. To be ecumenical means to reach out to others and seek unity with them through improved understanding. It does not mean to compromise on our beliefs. We cannot adequately share what we don't have. So it is only by learning our faith enough to love and defend it that we can reach out and share it with others.

If the task seems overwhelming, know that I too once felt unprepared. But deep down, I truly wanted to know my Faith. How else could I adequately represent my religion, fulfill my responsibilities as a loving parent, and provide my children with a solid Catholic foundation? For years, I put it off. When the nagging feeling grew too strong, I finally acknowledged to myself that my inability to hand down the Catholic faith to my children could have eternal consequences.

I began to read Catholic literature and educate myself on everything from the history of the Catholic Church and the sacraments to the lives of the saints and the role they can play in our lives. Rather than feeling bogged down with an unwieldy task, I experienced relief and excitement. For instance, I began to understand and appreciate the Church's seven sacraments. Instead of viewing Confession as unnecessary, I saw it as a divine invitation to forgiveness and grace given to us directly by Jesus through his apostles to strengthen our souls.

I shared many of the books I was reading with my husband, and we grew together in our faith. As we increased in our understanding of the Catholic Church, so too did our participation in the Church. Hindsight is twenty-twenty, and now we can see that much of the discord in our family was rooted in going our own way and forsaking God's way. We were like a ship adrift without a compass. Now, the Church is our compass, our guiding force. We fully accept that it's our responsibility to provide each of our eight children with this same compass to direct them through life's spiritual storms.

It is our God-given responsibility to teach our children the Faith. Even the Bible commands us: "Always be ready to give an explanation to anyone who asks you for a reason for your hope, but do it with gentleness and reverence, keeping your conscience clear, so that, when you are maligned, those who defame your good conduct in Christ may themselves be put to shame" (1 Pet 3: 15-16).

Ignorance of the law is never an excuse in a civil courtroom, so I suspect ignorance of our Faith will probably not excuse us in God's court. The task of really learning Catholicism may seem difficult at the outset, but the fruits of this labor are priceless. The rewards are the blessings God bestows on our families as we begin to practice our faith more adequately.

To pass down information, we teach it intellectually; but to get our children to integrate that knowledge into a belief system demands our own good example. That's why this book is written from one parent to another. Yes, we need to impart knowledge, but we also need to be living examples. That will speak louder to our children than any other lessons we give them,.

I started this spiritual journey of handing down the Catholic faith to my children with a mostly empty suitcase. But at least I started with a suitcase—my basic faith in God. I knew I needed something to put in the suitcase, and thus I began my research. So consider this book partly a travel log of the spiritual journey we are all on.

We will be packing items more valuable than anything in our closets. More precious than any family heirloom, money for college, or precious jewels is the pricelessness of our Catholic faith. My own eight children will come up fairly empty in terms of material inheritance. As meager as their material hand-me-downs will be, I want their spiritual inheritance to be rich and never-ending, for in the end, it will be all they really own. The richness of the world pales in comparison with spiritual treasures. This is why so many of the rich and famous lead unhappy, unfulfilled lives, while the poor and lowly, like Mother Teresa's Sisters of Charity, can fit all their earthly possessions into a bucket, yet the entire universe cannot contain the peace, love, and joy they hold in their hearts.

The thoughts, research, and love that went into this book are all I really have to hand down to my children, who are more valuable than any material good. We are all God's children, so we "parent together" as one body in Christ. Know that this book was written in prayer and love to share with you so that together we can all strive to pass down Catholic truths for our children.

1

AN IMPORTANT JOB

What's the most important thing you want to give your children? A college education? A generous inheritance? How about eternal happiness in heaven with God? Consider what is absolutely the most important thing in your children's lives. When you come up with bare bones priorities, loving and serving God and getting to heaven should be tops on the list.

Okay, now, look at your life. Where do you put most of your time and energy? An outside job? Driving to soccer, piano, and all the other practices? Television? Homework? Housework? If we let the pull of worldly things interfere with what should be our number one priority—raising our children for God and eternal happiness with Him—then we are blowing the whole point of having them in the first place. Not only is this our primary task, but it is wholly ours. Pope John Paul II proclaimed in his 1981 apostolic exhortation, "The Role of the Christian Family in the Modern World":

> The task of giving education is rooted in the primary vocation of married couples to participate in God's creative activity: by begetting in love and for love a new person who has within himself or herself the vocation to growth and development, parents by that very fact take on the task of helping that person effectively to live a fully human life. . . . The family is the first school of those social virtues which every society needs. The right and duty of parents to give education is essential since it is connected with the transmission of human life; it is original and primary with regard to the educational role of others . . . it is irreplaceable and inalienable, and therefore incapable of being entirely delegated to others or usurped by others. In addition to these characteristics, it cannot be forgotten that the most basic element, so basic that it qualifies

> the educational role of parents, is parental love, which finds fulfillment in the task of education. . . . As well as being a source, the parents' love is also the animating principle and therefore the norm inspiring and guiding all concrete educational activity, enriching it with the values of kindness, constancy, goodness, service, disinterestedness and self sacrifice that are the most precious fruit of love. . . .
>
> A vivid and attentive awareness of the mission that they have received with the sacrament of marriage will help Christian parents to place themselves at the service of their children's education with great serenity and trustfulness, and also with a sense of responsibility before God.

For me, the best way I can raise my children for God is to bring them up in His Church—the Roman Catholic Church. By giving our children something solid to hold on to and turn to, we can send them into the world as strong Christian soldiers, unwilling to trade in their faith and moral values for anything the world might offer.

If we do not fully teach our children to understand their Catholic faith, they may one day join the ranks of the thousands of lapsed Catholics or anti-Catholics who feel called upon to save others from what they believe is a dangerous institution—the Roman Catholic Church. There are books, magazines, and entire organizations set up for the very purpose of convincing Catholics to abandon their church. Our children need to recognize anti-Catholic criticisms and counter them or they risk being persuaded to leave the Church because they do not know the truth.

Some fundamentalist denominations actually devote a lot of their attention to trying to "evangelize" uninformed Catholics. They use Scripture taken out of context to support their attacks—even though it was the Catholic Church that compiled and preserved the Bible, long before there ever were any other Christian denominations.

Jesus gave his Church authority, and it was the authority of his Church that determined which sacred writings were of divine inspiration and therefore formed a part of the New Testament. The Catholic Church and Scripture are united. One will never disagree with the other.

Once people began breaking away from the one true Church and interpreting Scripture on their own, out of context, and with no authority, they began to come up with many false interpretations to claim the Catholic Church is in error.

These interpretations can seem persuasive to Catholics, raised in the faith, yet never fully understanding it. We all know fallen-away and ex-Catholics. They are often the most vehemently anti-Catholic. After all, they want to feel justified in leaving a faith they believe they discovered to be wrong.

I attended Catholic school for twelve years. Many of my former classmates and/or their many siblings have become apathetic to religion or antagonistic to Catholicism. When a former classmate who left the Church mistakenly thought I had also left, she told me, "Oh, I thought you had become Christian." I've had conversations with parents of fallen-away Catholics whose hearts ache while they wring their hands and ask, "What happened? We always took them to church," or "We paid for them to get a good Catholic education, a lot of good that did."

These experiences told me I needed to share my religion with my children to the point that it would truly become their own. The only problem was that when I developed this lofty goal, well over ten years ago, I became acutely aware of my own deficiencies as a Catholic. My level of understanding was not even enough for me to represent the Church to which I belonged.

Over the years I had been frustrated in debates with atheists, agnostics, non-Christians, and anti-Catholics. For instance, during a family reunion when my sister-in-law asked me why Catholics re-sacrifice Jesus at every Mass even though the Bible says his sacrifice on the cross was once and for all, I drew a blank. Another time, when an acquaintance questioned me as to why Catholics put Mary into their relationship with God in spite of the fact that the Bible says there is no mediator between God and Man but Jesus, again, I had no ready answer.

I found myself avoiding these arguments rather than giving my debaters fuel for feeling justified in attacking the Catholic Church. Not until my own children began growing older did I finally feel the need for definitive answers. I wanted to give them a faith that could arm them against the world's arguments that are so vehemently opposed to this "behind-the-times" institution—the Roman Catholic Church. Otherwise, how would my children grow up and tenaciously hold onto the religion of their parents? Could they be lured away by seeds of doubt—arguments they could not answer and answers that made sense in the absence of any contrary knowledge?

I had a responsibility to my children that in spite of twelve years of Catholic schooling in the 1960's and 1970's and more than thirty years as a Catholic, I was not prepared to fulfill. My children were growing and receiving the sacraments. I followed all the Church guidelines to prepare them, but the hard-core answers, the guts of our religion, still escaped my understanding and hence my ability to hand them down.

For instance, after preparing two sons for the sacrament of reconciliation (also known as penance and confession), I realized with my third son that I had never fully explained why Catholics receive this sacrament while other Christians do not. They were not learning enough to defend the virtues of this sacrament if attacked by non-Catholic friends. Other Christian faiths claim this sacrament is even blasphemous: ". . . There is one mediator between God and men, the man Christ Jesus" (1 Tim 2:5).

So where do Catholics get this notion of going to a priest to confess their sins? Other faiths go directly to Jesus like the Bible tells us to do. Right? I have posed this very question to many Catholic friends. Usually, they have no response. I didn't have one myself until almost twenty-five years after I made my own first confession.

In a nutshell (more on reconciliation later), Jesus forgave sins throughout his ministry, therefore, we know forgiveness of sins is important. Jesus also gave the apostles the power to forgive sins: "He breathed on them, and said to them, 'Receive the Holy Spirit. If you forgive the sins of any, they are forgiven; if you retain the sins of any, they are retained'" (Jn 20:22–23).

Just prior to that, in John 20:21, Jesus is sending the apostles out into the world to act in His place: "As the Father has sent me, even so I send you." The apostles were given the authority to act in Jesus' place because they were given leadership of his Church on earth. Catholics recognize the truth in 1 Timothy 2:5 (see above). Catholic confession does not contradict that, however. We do not confess our sins to a mere man, but to a priest who is standing in for Jesus. We are facing Jesus when we confess our sins, the same Jesus who promised us he would be with us until the end of the earth.

We learn humility in examining our consciences, confessing our sins, and receiving absolution. In Confession we also receive grace to help us avoid future sin, and to grow closer to God. It should be a treasured gift that we understand and use.

This is just an example of how understanding Church teaching more fully will empower us to share a deeper, fuller faith with our children. I elaborate on it here to illustrate the difference between just teaching our children *what* to do and *how* to do something as opposed to also explaining *why*.

As parents, what we need to do is teach our children to love and serve God through their Catholic faith. Why we need to do it is that it is our God given responsibility. How we need to do it is to learn all we can about our Catholic faith, teach it to our children at their age level, adding fuller explanations as they grow older. Finally, we must put our teachings into practice at home. If we want our children to go to confession, we should go. If we want our children to pray, we need to pray with them.

To shirk this responsibility means we fail to perform our God-given duty. If we try to convince ourselves we have enough faith so our children could make do with the same level of understanding, we again inadequately accomplish our task. Religious education classes and Catholic schools are supplements, but not the primary care givers of our children. Remember, Pope John Paul II said, "the family is the first school of virtues. . . ."

I believe it was my sense of a God-given responsibility that was nagging at me to learn about my religion. This record of my research is not intended to be a complete text. I have learned far more than I could include in this book, and I hope never to stop adding to that store of knowledge. I suggest getting into the habit of reading about the Catholic faith. History books, apologetics, conversion testimonials and stories about saints are a rich source of knowledge and inspiration. I would recommend getting a copy of the *Catechism of the Catholic Church*. As you grow in your faith, there will be many questions you want answered and so much more you will want to learn. The *Catechism* will be an important reference for you if it is not already.

In addition, Catholic literature for children is increasing in popularity. Older books are being republished, and new books are coming out all the time. You can begin reading Catholic Bible stories and lives of the saints' stories when your children are just toddlers. If you make up stories with your children, consider putting guardian angels in the cast of characters or have a main character stop to pray for guidance.

There are also many good audio books available nowadays. You might look into getting some audio books that can be played in the car when you are taking a trip that's a little longer than usual. Listening to a good book that is well read will not only use the time in an interesting way but will help make the trip seem shorter. If your parish has a lending library, it might have some good audio-book titles, or you could buy your own copies and share with other families with a similar interest.

Good video tapes likewise can help turn your television set into a "family friend." Many Catholic bookstores and distributors now offer a wide range of material; and many good videos are available for rental too. While television viewing should be kept at a minimum, it can be a tool for teaching your children the values of your family, as parenting author James Stenson points out in this way:

> Successful parents do not permit television or the other entertainment media to act as rivals for their children's respect and affection. They monitor and control what the family members watch at home. This is not done merely to shield the children (impossible in any event) but rather to express lessons of what is approved and what is not. Children thus see that the home is not open to persons and attitudes that offend the parents' principles.[1]

Suggestions are made throughout the book on how to present teachings to children. It is directed at parents with the belief

[1] James B. Stenson, *Upbringing: A Discussion Handbook for Parents of Young Children* (New York: Scepter, 1991), p. 52.

that once parents have firmly grasped the truths, they will be able to hand them down to their children. After I completed writing this book I went through it cover to cover with my children. I didn't read it word for word (although some sections were handled this way) but rather made sure each teaching with its Bible references was fully explained.

It's easy to teach Catholic truths to young children but teenagers sometimes "tune out". One technique I found helpful in this situation is to challenge them on their ability to defend Roman Catholicism. For instance ask them why they go to confession when in First Timothy it says there shall be no mediator between God and man, but Jesus? Why go to a mere man, the priest, to confess sins instead of going directly to Jesus? Ask your teenager to justify praying to Mary in view of the same passage in First Timothy. If there is a scandal in the Church in the news, ask your child how he can defend being Catholic in view of the scandal. How could this be Christ's Church?

If your kids know the answers to your questions, good for you. If they do not, you've primed them to be more attentive to the lesson since they just discovered they had no response to your challenge.

As I grew in understanding of my faith, the responsibility to teach my children felt more like a privilege. What a joy to be chosen by God to guide our young ones in the knowledge and love of God and foster a desire in them to be with him forever in heaven.

Recall the story of the rich man who approached Christ with the desire to improve himself even further than following the Ten Commandments (Mt 19:16–30): "Jesus said to him, 'If you would be perfect, go, sell what you possess and give to the poor, and you will have treasure in heaven; and come, follow me.' When the young man heard this, he went away sorrowful; for he had great possessions. . . . And every one who has left houses or brothers or sisters or father or mother or children or lands, for my name's sake, will receive a hundredfold, and inherit eternal life. But many that are first will be last, and the last first."

Jesus firmly tells us that we must put God at the center of our lives, but he promises us that the rewards will be great. God has chosen us to lead our children to him for everlasting happiness.

God demands complete faithfulness. We must not subordinate our religious faith and practice to worldly pleasures and concerns. Through prayer and faith in God's loving guidance, he leads us to himself:

> And so, from the day we heard or it, we have not ceased to pray for you, asking that you may be filled with the knowledge of his will in all spiritual wisdom and understanding, to lead a life worthy of the Lord, fully pleasing to him, bearing fruit in every good work and increasing in the knowledge of God. May you be strengthened with all power, according to his glorious might, for all endurance and patience with joy, giving thanks to the Father, who has qualified us to share in the inheritance of the saints in light. He has delivered us from the dominion of darkness and transferred us to the kingdom of his beloved Son, in whom we have redemption, the forgiveness of sins" (Col 1:9–14).

2

SQUARE ONE – GOD

The first building block in helping parents teach children the Catholic faith must be a firm belief in God. Our faith in God is the thread that connects us with most other religions, and it is at the core of our Catholic religion. The specifics of the Catholic Church's teachings are important, but without a rock-solid base—faith in God—everything else could crumble one day.

A close friend of mine from a good Catholic family began to question the very existence of God during her senior year of high school. Without that basic faith, nothing else pertaining to religion has had meaning for her. It has been twenty-five years, and she is still struggling. I hear from her from time to time, and she is in my prayers. She has recently assured me she will pray to receive the gift of faith, but she has trouble with that. She is not sure if anyone is listening.

There are too many people who discard faith in God as too unbelievable. They do not usually do it while they are very young and impressionable. After all, young children will believe in almost anything—like a guy in a red suit flying through the sky with reindeer to distribute presents to everyone. Instead, people often lose faith in God when they begin to contemplate the meaning of life, or question authority, or have a crisis of some sort in their lives. Some experience a loss in faith due to suffering or when prayers seem to go unanswered.

In the case of my friend, during a class on comparative religions we attended together, it struck her that each religion had its merits and each one thought it was right. Since the class never showed one religion as more Biblically and historically grounded than another, students were never guided to the truth of the Catholic Church. My friend began to feel there were no absolutes, no way of knowing the real truth, and no way of even knowing if there is a God. She began to fall into the common error that religions are nothing more than a lot of wishful and philosophical thinking by an assortment of groups who disagreed with one another.

Although faith is a gift, we can also teach it logically and experience it naturally with our children from the start. There is no need to wait until they are old enough for more formal instruction. We talk to our babies long before they can fully understand and talk back to us. Much of their initial learning happens this way. God should be a part of that early learning. He can be a part of their lives as far back as they can remember.

When you hold your child's hand and gaze at a magnificent sunset, pause together and give thanks to God for all the beautiful greetings he sends us. What other reason could there be for making snow that sparkles in the sun, flowers that indulge our sight and smell, rainbows that paint the sky and stars that twinkle in the night? Surely these are some of the ways God tells us, "I love you."

Enjoying the wonders of nature is one of the best ways to reinforce God's existence. Together with my children, I share my awe of the world God created for us. From the smallest insect or atom to the entire universe, everything is organized, intricate, and incredible. There must be a God. His handiwork is everywhere.

Making God real in your children's lives is the first step to believing in him and loving Him. Maybe for many atheists and agnostics, no one brought the wonder of God into their upbringing. If God were not made present to them growing up, then it was only a small step to believing he is not present at all. Likewise, if God is ever-present in childhood, it is less likely he will be abandoned one day. He will have been a part of our children's lives as far back as they can remember.

As our children grow in awareness and curiosity and begin to question life, the concept of God may seem confusing and incomprehensible to them at times. After all, God is incomprehensible. But let's not confuse comprehensible with believable. I find God totally incomprehensible but 100 percent believable.

Over the years my children have often raised questions in conversations: "But how can God exist? Who made Him?" They know I have no answer, because they are asking the ultimate question, the cornerstone of all faith in God. Yet, they ask it over and over.

I remember wondering the same thing. How could it be? How could a being exist infinitely in the past. Doesn't everything have a beginning? Who made God? Nothing can just make itself, so how could he have always existed? This article of faith certainly rests on faith alone, because there is no explanation of the infinite in our finite world.

Of course we must tell our children that it is a mystery, but we can help them to understand that it is an acceptable mystery by comparing it with the alternative—no faith in God. Help them to see that it is a misconception that some people have faith while others do not. All people have faith of some sort. It is merely a question of whether they believe in God or in something else far less logical.

Not everyone believes in God, but as human beings we are all persons of faith. Even atheists have faith. They have faith in nothing, a most daring, albeit wrong, faith. It is ironic that they who label the religious as superstitious or illogical have placed their faith in the most illogical philosophy of all.

While the God-fearing believe in God as our creator, those who don't believe in God certainly cannot deny that we do exist. Therefore, they must believe all life came from nothing. They have no faith in the existence of a creator. They have faith that there is nothing. We came from nothing and we are going nowhere. As illogical as this seems to believers, some well-educated people have believed this throughout history.

In spite of all the evidence that there is a God, I tell my children that faith is still a gift that some people, for whatever reason, lose. They learn that we must pray for nonbelievers because they probably do not pray for themselves. You can acknowledge how impossible it seems that so many bright minds are capable of missing God and show your children that God addresses this situation in the Bible:

> At that time Jesus declared, "I thank thee, Father, Lord of heaven and earth, that thou hast hidden these things from the wise and understanding and revealed them to babes" (Mt 11:25).

> Though he had done so many signs before them, yet they did not believe in him; it was that the word spoken by the prophet Isaiah might be fulfilled: "Lord, who has believed our report, and to whom has the arm of the Lord been revealed?" Therefore they could not believe. For Isaiah again said: "He has blinded their eyes and hardened their heart, lest they should see with their eyes and perceive with their heart, and turn for me to heal them" (Jn 12:37–40).

Even if we did not have the Bible or Jesus or the prophets, we could still know God exists. That is why so many early civilizations worshipped some sort of god or gods. Instinctively, they knew it could not be any other way. One only has to look at nature to know and believe that in spite of our inability to know how, he surely does exist.

I always begin with what we can know and see. We believe there has to be a Prime Mover that set life in motion. This Prime Mover must exist in and of itself, needing nothing outside itself to exist. This is God. God exists above the laws of nature. He made the laws of nature.

Human beings are the most intelligent life form on earth. We have survived by our wits over the years. We might not be able to climb the best or swim the fastest or fly, but we have survived by being able to solve problems and outsmart other creatures. Yet, as smart as we are, no human being has ever created anything totally by himself. We can use the raw materials and the intelligence and talents God gave us to create something new: a new invention, a cure for polio, or a new breed of honeybees. But we must always start with the raw materials God created. There is no way for us to create something out of nothing.

Ask your child if he can create something all by himself. A child might think of things he has made or mixed together, but, in the end, he will have to agree that if you put him in an empty room, it will remain empty. If your child thinks he has outsmarted you by saying he could spit, or blow his nose or somehow put something into the room, counter that everything that your body produces comes from something that has been put into it. Our bodies are only able to exist if we do put food and water in. And only God can put life into the very bodies he made and they can only continue to live if we take in the food and water that he also created.

Not only can we not make something from nothing, neither can we create life. Man has made robots that look and act almost human, but there is always an artificial power source, such as a battery or another electrical source. We can plant seeds and give them plenty of God's water, soil and sunlight, and they will grow, but we cannot personally create life. We can become parents, but that is the opportunity for us to cooperate with God's creation. Man has never been able to put life into the lifeless. It has never been done and it never will because only God can create life. Even in the case of cloning, man is attempting to create life from God's building blocks of life.

If you have already developed an appreciation for nature in your children, you can expand on it to enhance their understanding of creation. Nature is a force but it is a force with Someone behind it. It has no intelligence of its own. Nature is part of the divine plan. Nature did not make itself. Some say God is in all of nature, but as Catholics, we believe God created all nature but is above it.

Just as we cannot create anything alone, how could a planet create itself, give itself the right orbit, put itself the right distance from the sun, and cover itself with just the right atmosphere so life forms could breathe, at just the right temperature for life to exist and then keep it all together with something called gravity? How could all the mindless matter on this planet jumble together until, BINGO, life was formed?

Ask your child how complicated his wristwatch is, or the LEGO tower or science project he created. Is it more complicated than a living thing? Of course not. Now ask him to try putting all the parts of his watch or tower or project into a big bag and shake it all up until all the pieces have fallen into the right places. What are the odds? Yet, there are some people who think a bunch of mindless particles bubbling about in a warm pool of water eventually got together and just by chance, came alive. Atheists must know all these mindless things could not have just gotten there by themselves, but they accept that problem. They say the presence of the first building blocks of life is no more illogical than the presence of God.

We know that life is too impossibly complicated and incredible just to have happened by chance. How can the birds know how, when, and where to migrate? Who told them all? How do tiny, little, almost brainless ants, communicate, work together, build intricate homes, and survive winter?

Look at the bees. Who taught them to return to the hive and dance before the other bees in order to give intricate and specific directions when they discover a source of food? Consider any aspect of nature—clouds, colors, seeds, hibernations—and marvel at God's creation.

Consider water. Without it we would have no life. And if God had not arranged for water to break the natural order of things (contracting when it is cold and expanding when it is hot), the life cycle would be broken. If water at the top of ponds, rivers and lakes contracted when frozen, like other things do when they are cold, the ice would be heavier than the water, fall to the bottom, and kill all the marine life. So, instead, it expands and is able to float atop the water, thereby protecting the life below. God even changed his own laws of nature to make all things work together.

There are too many vital functions necessary for life to have had the luxury of evolving independently without a Supreme Being to orchestrate and make it possible. One cold North Dakota winter would be enough to wipe out all life forms if God did not give creatures the knowledge to survive, migrate or hibernate. There would not be the time to evolve this information on their own. If they did not get it right the first time, the flock, the herd, or the hive would all die.

It takes more than two dozen biochemical elements for blood to clot. If any one of them is not present, there will be no clotting. Imagine how long any species could survive without this ability. One mosquito bite and we would be in big trouble. Clotting could not have evolved on its own over thousands of years. It is irreducibly complex. Too many complicated abilities need to be fully intact from the start, or survival would be impossible.

So as not to confuse anyone, it is important to note here that I don't mean to infer that creationism, or a literal reading of the book of Genesis, is the norm in Catholic thinking. The Catholic Church does not hold to either strict creationism or evolution. The Church merely claims that however life came about, it did not happen without God. We believe that God is the author, creator, and governor of the universe but Catholic teaching allows for science to discover, if possible, the times, places, and modes of this origin.

Consider further how interdependent nature is. Where would we be without the food chain? We are 100 percent dependent on other life forms, even if our diet is vegetarian. How long can we go without eating and drinking? A few days maybe? God did not just make us, he made us very dependent. Perhaps he made us dependent on our parents as infants and children, so we could better understand our dependence on Him. "Whoever humbles himself like this child, he is the greatest in the kingdom of heaven" (Mt 18:4).

And maybe he kept us dependent even as adults on nature—a force we cannot completely control—so we would not forget our reliance on him. Understanding that we depend on God's gifts to keep us alive physically day by day helps us realize that we must also depend on him spiritually. Just as without food and water we cannot hope to survive for long, without prayer and a relationship with God, our souls cannot remain healthy.

It is important to explain this dependency as existing because of God's love for us. He wants to care for us, and he wants us to come to him to be cared for. God did not just surround us with food, he surrounded us with a variety so incredible as to forever delight our taste buds while providing health. And he made nature so simply beautiful and at the same time incomprehensibly complex as to dumbfound even the greatest minds through all of human history. He made the sun, the planets, and the universe to surround us in wonder and mystery.

Seeing God in nature and creation is a good start for nurturing faith in Him, but it will be meaningless if he is not present in your everyday family life. After all, it is illogical to claim there is a God who is the creator of the universe, who created us with the hope we would one day spend eternity in heaven with him, and then to ignore him for the most part. To make God real, we must acknowledge him regularly in our lives. Otherwise, television shows will seem more real than a God who is largely not acknowledged.

Young children will believe anything we tell them, from Santa Claus and tooth fairies to God. As they mature and get a firmer grasp on what is real and what is make believe, they can retain their faith in God under our guidance. It is our job not to drop the ball. For example, if we put more energy into Santa Claus—taking them to sit on his lap, telling the kids not to get on the naughty list, etc.—then when they discover he does not exist, where does that leave all the other things we have told them? If we want them to develop a strong faith in God, we need to make a bigger deal of him than of Santa, just as one example.

Making God present in our lives means regularly talking to him in prayer. If you are not accustomed to praying together or just expressing awe at God's creation, it might feel uncomfortable at first. We can remind ourselves that this is surely what God wants for our family—to make him the center of our lives—and we can be confident that if we ask, God will help us over this hurdle.

Begin talking to God throughout the day. Before your child tackles riding a two-wheeler, pray. When he comes to you with a skinned knee or a fever, pray for acceptance and healing. Don't send your child off to a big game or out to sell raffle tickets without praying first. When someone is frantically searching for a lost item, stop and pray. And when you get great news about something, pause and remember to thank God for his goodness.

The most natural place in the day to begin the prayer habit is in the morning, asking God to guide us through the day; at mealtime, thanking God for our food and asking him to bless it; and at bedtime, offering thanks for the day, sorrow for any wrongdoings, and asking help to improve.

If we are introducing prayers into the family schedule and some of the older children moan and groan, do not give up. Be clear and firm that God is the most important thing in your family's lives, and that we are incomplete without him. If your children display bad attitudes during prayer time, they are being disrespectful both to you and to God. As their parents, you would not be serving God and caring for the children he entrusted to you if you allow this.

For older children, not accustomed to regular family prayer time, you might offer this simple explanation: "Turning to God in prayer throughout the day benefits our family, so we've decided to say evening and morning prayers together." Bible reading, memorized prayers, spontaneous prayers, and singing are all ways to draw closer and communicate directly with God as well as being open to listening to what he wants to tell us.

Younger children will respond easily by following our lead. Most older children will too, but if there are rough spots with teenagers, persevere. I think it would be a mistake to let an older child claim he will say his prayers on his own in the privacy of his room. You should support his need to have private time with God. But be firm about family prayers—a time the family comes together to contemplate and speak with God as a unit. Prayer is the spiritual cement that bonds families together.

In times of trouble or happiness, it will become second nature for our children to talk to God. My children have told me that whenever they hear an ambulance siren, they pray on their own if I am not around. I had told them of remembering hearing a siren as a little girl and that my dad said we should always pray for that person needing help. I said a prayer then and for every siren since. It was a short, one-time comment that has now been handed down through generations.

While praying makes God present in our lives, we need to help our children develop an in depth understanding of prayer. They must know that prayers are important because they bring us closer to God and protect us from evil. Young children easily pray to God with unwavering faith, confident that he hears their prayers. At some point in their lives, however, regardless of how strong their prayers are, they will feel their pleas were not answered. We need to help them understand that God does hear their prayers but at times gives them something else, which he sees is better for them.. Or maybe he is saying, not yet. A shallow understanding of prayer often leads people to wonder, "What's the point?" Occasionally, even adults, with a solid faith, can be tempted to feel their prayers are not answered.

Teaching acceptance of prayers not answered according to our desires goes hand in hand with teaching an acceptance of suffering. At times I have heard people say something to the effect, "How could there be a God when this sort of suffering happens?" While volunteering as a counselor for unwed pregnant girls, I once had a girl tell me she stopped believing in God after she saw an uncle go through prolonged suffering. When I told her I would pray for her, she said not to bother with her but that I could pray for her unborn baby. I responded that her baby needed a good mother so I would also pray for her. Clearly, not only was her original faith in God shallow, but, fortunately, so too was her atheism.

Another example of shallow faith occurred during my high school years. One Monday morning students were grieved to hear there had been a serious car accident after a Sunday afternoon football game. A sophomore girl died in the crash. I clearly remember one of her classmates crying in the bathroom and claiming that if a young girl could die like that, then there could be no God. Attempts by other students to convince her otherwise fell on deaf ears.

The temptation to despair is especially strong at times when prayer fails to relieve intense or relentless suffering. Because suffering sometimes makes people question the existence or the goodness of God, I believe helping our children accept life's suffering is an essential part of their faith in God. They need answers to questions such as, "If God loves us, why does he let us suffer?" Or, "I keep praying, so why isn't God answering me?" This is a more difficult subject to tackle than teaching our children to pray to a God who loves us.

Our relationship with God can either be strengthened or strained during suffering. Early training can help determine which it will be. When my children struggle with some difficulty, I often tell them that we suffer because this is not heaven. They know the story of Adam and Eve and that because sin entered the world so too did suffering. I commiserate with them when they ask, "Why did they have to disobey God?" I also point out that each of us have sinned many times, so what's the likelihood that we would have passed the same test?

Any talk about suffering should include an explanation that there is disorder in this world as a consequence of Original Sin, but we have eternal happiness to look forward to. The topic of suffering comes up periodically in our family. My children often ask questions like, "Why do we have to suffer? Why do we get sick?" And my favorite: "Why do you think God made mosquitoes?" I explain that suffering is part of life in this world because we ignore the loving guidelines God gives us. We foolishly disobey his commandments and bring suffering on ourselves. And people suffer far more than they need when they do not stay close to God. None of us need suffer alone, and we are silly if we do so. God will comfort us when we are hurt and save us from much needless pain if we let him guide our lives.

We should also point out that while suffering is not good in itself, it can be good for us. Many people become deeper, more sensitive, more mature, and happier when they go through periods of suffering. We can also point out that the two people that God loved most, his own Son and his Blessed Mother, went through intense suffering, and probably all of the saints did also. Suffering is a way of saving souls, the souls of the persons who suffer and the souls of those for whom they offer up their suffering. At Lourdes and at Fatima our Lady asked the young visionaries again and again to do penance to save souls.

Teach and show your children how they must go to God in prayer for comfort and acceptance during difficult times. Share your own disappointments and sufferings with your children in a way that will impact them positively. Of course you don't want to burden them with worries beyond their maturity but let them see you accepting and praying for strength during difficult times. During the times when we are struggling with an aspect of life not of our own choosing, we should do it with faith, confident that God understands our difficulties and is helping us carry our burdens. Scripture says:

> Blessed be the God and Father of our Lord Jesus Christ, the Father of mercies and God of all comfort, who comforts us in all our affliction, so that we may be able to comfort those who are in any affliction, with the comfort with which we ourselves are comforted by God. For as we share abundantly in Christ's sufferings, so through Christ we share abundantly in comfort too (2 Cor 1:3–5).

> My grace is sufficient for you, for power is made perfect in weakness (2 Cor 12:9).

> "Come to me, all who labor and arc heavy laden, and I will give you rest. Take my yoke upon you, and learn from me; for I am gentle and lowly in heart; and you will find rest for your souls. For my yoke is easy and my burden is light" (Mt 11:28–30).

The reasons for our suffering are not always obvious, but just as parents have a broader view of life than their children, so too, God sees our future more clearly than we do. God sees our future as including eternity. So, we must trust him to know what is best for us. I also tell my children that God sent his own Son to suffer in our place in order to open the gates of heaven. This realization—Christ's suffering for us—helps me to accept my own hardships. Suffering is a consequence of original sin and our own weakness, but it takes on meaning if we unite ourselves and our suffering to the suffering of Jesus.

Teach your children to trust in God. He has our best interests at heart. We are precious to Him.

> "Are not two sparrows sold for a penny? And not one of them will fall to the ground without your Father's will. But even the hairs on your head are all numbered. Fear not, therefore; you are of more value than many sparrows" (Mt 10:29–31).

To present this lesson in a positive light, consider that anything worth having is worth working for. We must work for heaven and accept life's trials and difficulties. Learning to walk and to ride a bike was not easy for our children. They fell, got hurt, and became frustrated. But the prize was worth the suffering, and in the end they conquered. When we give our children consequences for bad behavior, it means they suffer in some way. The purpose, however, is to make them stronger and better individuals. These are all little rewards compared to eternal happiness in heaven with God.

> But, as it is written, "What no eye has seen, nor ear heard, nor the heart of man conceived, what God has prepared for those who love him" (1 Cor 2:9).

The best news, of course, is that suffering is not the end of the story. After Christ suffered his passion and death, he rose glorious and triumphant from the dead on the third day. Just as there is always a happy ending in fairy tales, our life with God will be the happy ending to end all happy endings.

> If we have died with him, we shall also live with him; if we endure, we shall also reign with him (2 Tim 2: 11–12).
>
> But rejoice in so far as you share Christ's sufferings, that you may also rejoice and be glad when his glory is revealed (1 Pet 4: 13).

3

THE TRINITY AND THE INCARNATION

A. *Three Persons in One God*

When we talk to our young children about God, and then also talk about Jesus and the Holy Spirit, there may be some confusion. Is there more than one God? What does it mean when we say, "In the name of the Father and of the Son and of the Holy Spirit?" Is baby Jesus God's Son? How is the God of Moses and Abraham connected to Jesus and the Holy Spirit?

At some point in teaching children about God, we need to explain that there are three persons in one God—the Father, Son, and Holy Spirit. I have always thought that the Trinity was a complicated concept and once asked my kids, "It's hard to understand isn't it?" My children claimed it made sense to them. This response surprised me at first, but it also got me thinking.

I recalled being taught in first grade that three persons in one God was a mystery. My teacher went on at length about it being a divine mystery we cannot understand. I recall distinctly thinking, "What's so mysterious? It makes perfect sense to me."

Now as an adult, the Trinity is far more complicated than I once thought. Sometimes our children's tendency to believe and accept anything seems like a trait they need to outgrow. But when you consider how open they are to our teachings about God and religion, it is clear this is a gift parents need to take advantage of by filling their minds with good teaching. Just as a sapling is easy to bend to the shape in which we desire it to grow, so our children's flexible imaginations can be guided along right paths. As their cognitive abilities deepen and expand, they will crave additional information to be added to the basic lessons we start them on. But as their thinking becomes their own, the roots of their faith will blossom into maturity. So don't fret if the Trinity seems an overwhelming lesson to you; our children might not find it so complicated at first.

We can teach our children that there is only one God. Other religions believe in God, but not everyone believes that God consists of God the Father, God the Son, and God the Holy Spirit. The three divine Persons in God are called the Blessed Trinity. In Genesis, there is reference to God being more than one person: "Then God said, "Let us make man in our image, after our likeness" (Gen 1:26).

The angel Gabriel revealed the Trinity at the Annunciation. St. Gabriel referred to all three Persons: "The Holy Spirit will come upon you and the power of the Most High will overshadow you; therefore the child to be born will be called holy, the Son of God" (Lk 1:35).

At Jesus' baptism, the Trinity was revealed publicly: "When Jesus also had been baptized and was praying, the heaven was opened, and the Holy Spirit descended upon him in bodily form, as a dove, and a voice came from heaven, 'Thou art my beloved Son; with thee I am well pleased' " (Lk 3:21–22).

After the resurrection Jesus sent his apostles out into the world to preach and baptize in the Trinity: "Go therefore and make disciples of all nations, baptizing them in the name of the Father and of the Son and of the Holy Spirit" (Mt 28:19).

In his mission work to Ireland, tradition has it that St. Patrick used a three-leafed clover or shamrock to show that even though there were three leaves, there was still only one plant. God the Father is the First Person of the Blessed Trinity. Jesus Christ is the Son of God, the Second Person of the Blessed Trinity. He is also referred to as the Word or Image of the Father. "In the beginning was the Word, and the Word was with God, and the Word was God" (Jn 1:1). The Holy Spirit is God, the Third Person of the Blessed Trinity. The Holy Spirit is also called the Holy Ghost, the Spirit, the Advocate and the Paraclete.

The three divine persons are distinct from one another. The Father is not the Son and the Son is not the Holy Spirit. Even though the three divine Persons are really distinct from one another, they are still one and the same God because they share the same divine nature.

Because of our faith in God, we accept this truth as a

supernatural mystery, which means we can never fully understand it. Using the Bible, we can show our children that God reveals to us that there are three persons in one God. So we can believe it, even though we are incapable of understanding it.

God the Father, the First Person in the Trinity, is mentioned by Jesus throughout the New Testament. Jesus frequently refers to God as his Father, showing us that he is a distinct Person, separate from his Father, yet still part of the one God. We too can call God our Father in Heaven, but for us it is different. We are God's creatures; Jesus was also God. Below are just four of the many Bible passages where Jesus refers to his Father making it clear that the Father is a separate person from the Son:

> But Jesus answered them, "My Father is working still, and I am working." That was why the Jews sought all the more to kill him, because he not only broke the sabbath but also called God his father, making himself equal with God (Jn 5:17–18).
>
> "But of that day and hour no one knows, not even the angels of heaven, nor the Son, but the Father only" (Mt 24:36).
>
> "All things have been delivered to me by my Father; and no one knows who the Son is except the Father, or who the Father is except the Son and any one to whom the Son chooses to reveal him" (Lk 10:22).
>
> Jesus cried out in a loud voice, "Father, into your hands I commit my spirit!" (Lk 23:46).

I am going to skip ahead to the Third Person of the Trinity—the Holy Spirit. Because belief in Jesus as God is the crucial point that separates Christians from non-Christians, I take much more time in discussing him as God and will do that last in a separate section.

According to Pope John Paul II, the Holy Spirit is "the center of Christian faith" and "a dynamic power of the Church's renewal" (*Dominum et Vivificantem*). We refer to the Holy Spirit in the Nicene Creed as "the giver of life." It is the Holy Spirit who gives life to our faith. The Holy Spirit allows our faith to grow and come alive. It becomes a faith not just on paper or in our head, but alive in our hearts: "Do you not know that you are God's temple and that God's Spirit dwells in you?" (1 Cor 3:16).

It is the Holy Spirit whom Jesus promised to send to keep his Church in truth: "Nevertheless I tell you the truth: it is to your advantage that I go away, for if I do not go away, the Counselor will not come to you; but if I go, I will send him to you" (Jn 16:7). "But when the Spirit of truth comes, he will guide you into all the truth" (Jn 16:13).

Before Jesus ascended into heaven, he promised his apostles: "But you will receive power when the Holy Spirit has come upon you . . ." (Acts 1:8). For nine full days, the apostles and Blessed Mother waited and prayed. (This is where the custom of the novena—nine days of prayer—came from). On the tenth day a sound like a great wind was heard. Then what appeared to be tongues of fire settled on each of them (Acts 2:3). This was the visible manifestation of the descent of the Holy Spirit that Jesus had promised. This day is known as Pentecost Sunday, celebrated as the birthday of the Church. From that point on, the scared, hiding apostles became Spirit-filled missionaries; full of courage, zeal, and understanding.

The crowd that had gathered outside was initially attracted by the noise. When the apostles, beginning with St. Peter, began to preach, all understood them in their native tongues, although they were from many countries. Three thousand were converted that day. Three thousand! It was truly the work of the Holy Spirit. It is to the Holy Spirit I pray that my children will burn with zeal for love of God and have the courage to live their beliefs.

B. *God the Son, True God and True Man*

The Second Person of the Trinity, Jesus, personalizes God for us. God is not some remote creator in the sky, removed from everyday life. Jesus became one of us in order to save us. He suffered and died for our sins. He loves us that much and is that personally involved in our lives. By reading about Jesus and listening to his teachings in the New Testament, God's love becomes real to us.

Jesus is the only Person to be both God and man: "And the Word became flesh and dwelt among us, full of grace and truth;

we have beheld his glory, glory as of the only Son from the Father" (Jn 1:14). His name in Hebrew means "God saves."

He has the same divine nature as God but is also man because he "became flesh" when he was conceived in the womb of the Blessed Mother by the power of the Holy Spirit. The Son becoming man is known as the Incarnation—the most important event in human history. We believe that Jesus, the Son of God, is our Savior who became man, died for our sins, rose from the dead, ascended into heaven and will return in glory to judge the living and the dead.

By his death on the cross and his resurrection, he freed us from sin and death. Jesus is our Redeemer. His sufferings and death were a sacrifice in satisfaction for the sins of men and regained for us the right to be called children of God and inherit the kingdom of heaven: *"For God so loved the world that he gave his only Son, that whoever believes in him should not perish but have eternal life"* (Jn 3:16).

The Bible records the Angel Gabriel announcing to the Blessed Virgin Mary that she is to be the Mother of God. It tells of his birth in a manger, the visits of the shepherds and wise men, his circumcision and presentation in the temple, Mary and Joseph's flight into Egypt and subsequent return, and his remaining in the Temple at the age of twelve. After Mary and Joseph searched for three days, and then found Jesus in the midst of the teachers, he returned with them to Nazareth. Even though Jesus told Mary and Joseph, "Did you not know that I must be in my Father's house?" he was obedient to them and returned home. The last we hear of his childhood is: "And Jesus increased in wisdom and in stature, and in favor with God and man" (Lk 2:52). Fr. Leo Trese, in his book *The Faith Explained*, says that

> Jesus was teaching us during his hidden years at Nazareth one of the most important lessons that man has need of. By quiet year piled upon quiet year, he was impressing upon us the fact that before God no person is unimportant and no task is trivial.
>
> It is not by the size of our job that God measures us, but rather by the fidelity with which we try to do the thing

> that he has placed in our hands to do—the wholeheartedness with which we try to make his will ours.

The next time we hear from Jesus, he is thirty years old. Jesus taught and performed miracles for only about three years, and yet his influence has changed the world. Even if you didn't believe in Jesus' divinity, as an objective historian you would have to admit that the impact this carpenter had on the world is unsurpassed by anything or anyone before or since.

Still, there are plenty of people who deny that Jesus was the Son of God. Many religions that believe in God claim that Jesus was merely a prophet, or just a good man. In teaching my children about Jesus, I make a strong impact by borrowing an argument put forth by Anglican writer C. S. Lewis. He maintained that if Jesus was, in reality, just a mere man, then he had to have been a very bad man. If he were only a man, and not God, then he was the biggest con artist who ever lived, faking miracles and blaspheming God.

Some New Age religions consider Jesus only one of many great philosophers and teachers. It is possible to believe this only if one is ignorant of history. We base our beliefs on the historical document of the New Testament. These original writings do exist in their entirety. As one writer notes:

> . . . but there have been cataloged some 4,280 very old manuscripts or fragments of manuscripts of the New Testament. . . . Not one of the ancient Latin or Greek classics is supported by as much manuscript evidence as is the New Testament."[1]

Before Jesus began his ministry, John the Baptist announced his coming, " . . . he who is coming after me is mightier than I" (Mt 3:11). When John baptized Jesus, his identity is revealed from heaven: "And lo, a voice from heaven, saying, 'This is my beloved Son, with whom I am well pleased' " (Mt 3:17).

Teaching was the core of Jesus' ministry. He came in love, as the Good Shepherd. He taught us doctrines for men to follow in

[1]Alexander, *College Apologetics*, p. 47. For photostats, see W. H. P. Hatch, *The Principal Uncial Manuscripts* (Univ. of Chicago Press, 1939).

order to avail themselves of the fruits of the redemption he won for us. He said: "I am the good shepherd. The good shepherd lays down his life for the sheep" (Jn 10:11).

> "For the Son of man also came not to be served but to serve, and to give his life as a ransom for many" (Mk 10:45).
>
> "He who believes in the Son has eternal life; he who does not obey the Son shall not see life, but the wrath of God rests upon him" (Jn 3:36).

As Jesus' ministry unfolds, he gradually makes it clear to his followers that he is not only doing the work of God, but he is also God, the Son:

> "For this is the will of my Father, that every one who sees the Son and believes in him should have eternal life; and I will raise him at the last day. . . . No one can come to me unless the Father who sent me draws him; and I will raise him at the last day. It is written in the prophets: 'And they shall all be taught by God.' Every one who has heard and learned from the Father comes to me. Not that any one has seen the Father except him who is from God; he has seen the Father. Truly, truly, I say to you, he who believes has eternal life" (Jn 6:40–47).

Jesus made the claim, over and over:

> "I and the Father are one" (Jn 10:30).
>
> ". . . the Father is in me and I am in the Father" (Jn 10:38).
>
> "He who has seen me has seen the Father" (Jn 14:9).

So, Jesus claimed to be the Son of God, but did he prove it? Yes, he did. Over and over he proved it. As the *Catechism of the Catholic Church* points out (no. 447), "Throughout his public life, he demonstrated his divine sovereignty by works of power over nature, illness, demons, death, and sin." Anyone could say he was the Son of God and claim to forgive sins, but only God can predict the future, which Jesus did several times when he predicted his own death and resurrection.

> "For as Jonah was three days and three nights in the belly of the whale, so will the Son of man be three days and three nights in the heart of the earth" (Mt 12:40).

> As they were gathering in Galilee, Jesus said to them, "The Son of Man is to be delivered into the hands of men, and they will kill him, and he will be raised on the third day" (Mt 17:22–23).

Jesus predicted his passion a third time (Mt 20:18) and also predicted Peter's denial (Mt 26:34).

Some people insist that Jesus was a bogus faith healer. They claim that people were hypnotized into believing he was performing miracles. That sort of thing has been done before. Mass hysteria can also lead crowds to jump to false conclusions. But how could Jesus fake turning a withered hand whole? How could a man blind at birth convince himself he sees? Can a leper be hypnotized into healing his body? Some stubborn unbelievers would say the mind is a powerful instrument. You can't hypnotize the dead, however. And on three occasions, Jesus raised the dead to life: Lazarus (Jn 11:1–44), a widow's son (Lk 7:11–17), and a young girl (Mt 9:25).

Also recall that Jesus fed a crowd of five thousand with five loaves and two fish (Mt 14:13–21). It would be pretty difficult to fool that many people into thinking they have eaten, and how would you account for the twelve baskets of leftovers?

What kind of trickery could have convinced the disciples to see Jesus walking on water and allow Peter also to walk on water? "And those in the boat worshiped him, saying, 'Truly you are the Son of God'" (Mt 14:33).

Do you know anyone but God who can calm down a raging storm in a hurry?

> . . . Who then is this, that he commands even wind and water, and they obey him? (Lk 8:25).

During Christ's time on earth, as well as today, many have difficulty accepting Jesus as God, but it is interesting that those possessed by demons had no trouble knowing exactly who Jesus was. As one demonic announced: "What have you to do with me, Jesus, son of the Most High God? I beseech you, do not torment me!" (Lk 8:28).

If your faith in Jesus Christ, Son of God, is firmly planted, perhaps all above examples seem overdone to you. Your children will not be bored with these stories, however. They are many times better than any superhero cartoon. Jesus is the hero in these amazing but true stories. He is the good guy with the only truly superhero powers, the ones from God.

The best part about Jesus is that he is God, and yet he became one of us. He must really love us to have gone through all the trouble of being born a baby, possessing all the humanness that we ourselves possess. How could God, the creator of the universe, the all-knowing eternal being, choose to become one of us? Jesus is not only God, he is our friend. If we let him, he will be one with us.

The stories in the New Testament don't just teach our children about Jesus, they also teach them to love him. How could they not? Read the story of Jesus' passion in the four Gospels. Contemplate his suffering and crucifixion at the hands of malicious and ignorant men and then contemplate Jesus' unfathomable greatness as the Son of God. How could he have humbled himself so? We have trouble handling it well if someone calls us a mean name. How did God allow himself to be tortured, feeling all the same pain any human body would under the same circumstances? He did it for only one reason: he loves us. The more our children know about Jesus, the more they will love Him, because he loved us first.

Thus John Paul II (*Novo Millennio Ineunte*, no. 15): "If we ask what is the core of the great legacy it [the Millennial celebration] has left us, I would not hesitate to describe it as the contemplation of the face of Christ: Christ considered in his historical features and in his mystery, Christ known through his manifold presence in the Church and in the world, and confessed as the meaning of history and the light of life's journey."

> Though he was in the form of God, [he] did not regard equality with God a thing to be grasped, but emptied him-

> self, taking the form of a servant, being born in the likeness of men. And being found in human form, he humbled himself and became obedient unto death, even death on a cross. Therefore God has highly exalted him and bestowed on him the name which is above every name" (Phil 2:6–8).

To arm your children with more convincing evidence of the authenticity of Jesus' claim to be God, have them consider the events after his death. On Good Friday, Jesus' enemies achieved their goal. Jesus died on the cross after much physical and mental abuse:

> When the centurion and those who were with him, keeping watch over Jesus, saw the earthquake and what took place, they were filled with awe, and said, "Truly this was the Son of God!" (Mt 27:54).

As the redeemer of the whole human race, Jesus offered his sufferings and death to God the Father in satisfaction for the sins of men and opened heaven to us. As the Apostles' Creed says, after Jesus died, "He descended into hell" or, in another version, "He descended to the dead." This means Jesus descended to the place of rest where the souls of the just were waiting for him to be brought to heaven. Jesus' resurrection from the dead meant he had returned to life. His soul was reunited to his body, and he appeared on earth for forty days before ascending into heaven.

The Pharisees remembered Christ's prediction that he would rise after three days, so they placed guards at his tomb. Early Easter morning, the third day, something like an earthquake frightened the guards. When they recovered they saw that the stone had been rolled away, revealing an empty tomb:

> And when they had assembled with the elders and taken counsel, they gave a sum of money to the soldiers and said, "Tell people, 'His disciples came by night and stole him away while we were asleep'" (Mt 28:12–13).

If there had been an unrisen body, the Pharisees would have stopped at nothing to have produced it and put an end to this new religion. If they had had a shred of evidence to prove Jesus was a fraud, they would have produced it. There is historical evidence of unbelief among Jesus' contemporaries, but there is not a single historical document containing evidence that Jesus was a fraud.

The Pharisees accused Jesus' followers of perpetuating a fraud, but it is interesting that the accused—the would-be scam artists—had no inkling of the full extent of Jesus' prediction of his resurrection. Even though Jesus had talked to his apostles several times about rising from the dead, they never really understood him. St. Mark records:

> He was teaching his disciples, saying to them, "The Son of man will be delivered into the hands of men, and they will kill him; and when he is killed, after three days he will rise." But they did not understand the saying, and they were afraid to ask him (Mk 9:31–32).

All the apostles but John fled in fear when Jesus was condemned to death and crucified. Early on Easter Sunday morning, some of the women went to the tomb with spices to complete the embalming. They expected to find a body, but instead found an angel who announced that Jesus had risen. The apostles were as surprised as anyone by this story, and they refused to believe it. Until Jesus himself appeared that evening to the apostles, they were not convinced. Even after the women and the apostles testified that Jesus had risen, Thomas, who was absent that evening, would not accept it until Jesus appeared personally to him and the other apostles a week later. On seeing Christ and touching the wounds in his hands and side Thomas made a big act of faith: "My Lord and my God!" he exclaimed. But Jesus said to him, "Have you believed because you have seen me? Blessed are those who have not seen and yet believe" (Jn 20:29).

The apostles were cowards at this time, certainly not bold conspirators of a scam. They themselves, Jesus' own handpicked followers, did not believe in His resurrection until he showed himself to them. And yet, once they understood all that Jesus had been trying to teach them and received courage from the Holy Spirit on Pentecost Sunday, they went out and boldly preached about Jesus. All but John were eventually put to death for their teaching. Tradition tells us that John was arrested and condemned to death. He was put in a cauldron of boiling oil but miraculously survived it. He was then exiled to the island of Patmos, where he wrote the Apocalypse. Eventually he returned to Ephesus, where he died at an advanced age.

The apostles were accused of spreading lies, continuing the hysteria begun by Jesus, and misleading the people. If this were true, it would have made the apostles a bunch of phonies, trying to cover up the fact that their leader turned out to be a false messiah. But these men were willing to die for their belief in Jesus. People do not die for something they do not believe in.

There is more historical evidence for Jesus' resurrection than many of the historical events we take for granted. The earliest document we have is the Epistle to the Corinthians by St. Paul, written in A.D. 55, only 25 years after the Resurrection. The first three Gospels accounts were written in the 60's, as close (or closer) to the event they were describing than Herodotus the Greek historian was to the Battle of Marathon. Matthew and John were eyewitnesses to the event, and we know that Mark received the data for his accounts directly from a third eyewitness, Peter.

The Gospels refer by name to many people who were still alive or were known to those who were, such as Joseph of Arimathea, but none of these people appeared to contest the data. We have no record that any of the Jewish leaders presented evidence proving the Gospels false. If there were any such evidence, they certainly would have produced it because of the inroads Christianity was making among the Jews. Instead they kept silence.

St. Paul gives an account of witnesses to Jesus' resurrection:

> . . . that he appeared to Cephas, then to the twelve. After that, he appeared to more than five hundred brethren at on time, most of whom are still alive, though some have fallen asleep. Then he appeared to James, then to all the apostles (1 Cor 15:5–7).

It was not just the accounts of the apostles that convinced the ever-growing number of converts. Through the power of God, the apostles continued to perform miracles and expel demons, and they spoke with the force of the Holy Spirit. Not even the threat of death could stop the growth of Christianity. It is now an almost two thousand-year-old faith that continues to grow and one that people continue to die for in countries where Christianity is persecuted.

Jesus was no mere man. He is the Savior of the World, he is God, and best of all, he loves us enough to have died for us.

4

WHY A CHURCH?

Thus far we have discussed believing in and knowing God. So do we really need anything more? Why should we belong to a specific church? Can't we just believe in God and live good and holy lives?

Many people who believe in God do not see the importance of belonging to a church. Some are cynical about organized churches. They may turn instead to their Bibles, or a short family devotion, or they may not participate in any religious observance for the most part. If you have noticed the fluctuating crowds at Mass, particularly obvious every Christmas and Easter, then you know many Catholics do not feel it is important to follow the Sunday Mass requirement. Perhaps you are such a Catholic, seeing obligations to a particular church as unnecessarily cumbersome to spiritual life.

Aside from missing all that Mass offers us, there are flaws in this way of thinking. We need the Church. Jesus told us so and it is also written in the Bible. Nowhere does Scripture encourage people to go off on their own. It is clear from the teachings of Jesus and the Bible that we are to be a part of a community—the Church:

> And let us consider how to stir up one another to love and good works, not neglecting to meet together, as is the habit of some, but encouraging one another (Heb 10:24–25).

> "I am the vine, you are the branches. He who abides in me, and I in him, he it is that bears much fruit, for apart from me you can do nothing. If a man does not abide in me, he is cast forth as a branch and withers; and the branches are gathered, thrown into the fire and burned" (Jn 15:5–6).

It is very flimsy ground to say you are living in Christ and are connected to him—the vine—while staying away from organized religion or church membership. As part of the "One Body," the Church on earth with Christ as the head, we need to join together. Members of a body are part of one another, they belong together:

> For as in one body we have many members, and all the members do not have the same function, so we, though many, are one body in Christ, and individually members one of another (Rom 12:4).

As a family or "body," the sailing is not always smooth. Brothers and sisters and parents do not always find it easy to get along and sometimes the parts of our body do not act in agreement. When I want to go jogging, my forty-plus-year-old knees remind me that my heart and mind might like the idea, but there is another body part that might not cooperate. Maybe you love spicy food or crave chocolate, but your digestive system rebels.

If our own families and bodies do not always perform smoothly as a unit, why should we be surprised that "one body in Christ," the Church, encounters discord among its members. Does that mean we should go our own way and do our own thing? What kind of a family splits apart? A dysfunctional one. What kind of a body has parts of it surgically separated from the whole? An ailing one.

Jesus wants us to belong to his Church, his body. We cannot baptize ourselves or give ourselves the sacraments. Without participating in weekly Mass, we miss the opportunity to receive the Eucharist. Jesus wants us to gather and not go it alone. "For where two or three are gathered in my name, there am I in the midst of them" (Mt 18:20).

Without the Church, how do you know you are interpreting the Bible as God intended? So much of the New Testament is based on the fulfillment of the Old. Much of the Old Testament foretells events in the New. We are not all experts on history, geography, languages and the customs of various ethnic groups mentioned in the Bible. How can we pride ourselves in being able to interpret such a complicated book and know Catholic teaching? "The Holy Spirit will interpret," many claim. If the Holy Spirit is interpreting for so many, why is it that, as of 1980, in the Church Book of World Religions, more than 18,000 Christian denominations are listed? Each splintering of the Christian faith stems from a disagreement over Bible interpretation.

But look at all the corruption that comes from institutional churches, many cry! How do you respond when people bring up all the evils of the past? Or what do you say to someone who points to the latest "priest scandal" the media is all fired up about? Scandals will occur both inside and outside of churches. To point to someone's misdeeds as a reason for staying away from organized churches is faulty rcasoning.

Let me digress just a moment to say I think it is a mistake to avoid teaching our children about scandals in our long history. I know firsthand, because I entered college without a clue that the Catholic Church had been anything other than the model of perfection.

Sitting in my Michigan State University humanities class at the age of twenty, I was horrified to learn of the selling of indulgences and some of the greed and corruption Church officials fell prey to. How could all this have been hidden from me for so long? I spent twelve years at a Catholic school and only then, in that humanities class did something a nun said years earlier make sense to me. Sr. Willard was the only one who ever even alluded to the fact that there was anything not completely virtuous in our history. She had several times referred to the Church's past and said, "We just have to have faith even when it's hard." She looked troubled whenever she said it, and I wasn't quite sure what she was getting at—until my humanities class bombshell.

I felt betrayed to learn of the scandals for the very first time in college. There was no one to explain it to me in the context of the Catholic Church. I wasn't traveling in Catholic circles. There was no one around to provide a context for the dark side of Church history. My shattered image of the Church led to cynicism. The Church seemed a lot less holy, a lot less perfect and a lot less necessary in my life.

It would have been better for my teachers to have tackled corruption head on. To send Catholics out into the world without breaking the "whole story" to us was like not telling someone he is adopted, or learning of a betrayal from a third party. I wonder how many others have felt betrayed like me and just left the Church?

How much you want to teach your children is up to you, but I would certainly wait until they are older and have a firm grasp on the truths of the Roman Catholic faith. However much we choose to tell them, we can explain that men and women are sinners and institutions are made up of people, even the Church that Jesus founded. This, however, is not a reason to turn away from the institutional church. Jesus founded this Church for us, to strengthen us, to give of himself. The fact that there will be sinful as well as holy people in the Church does not mean that we should shun Jesus' gift to us.

Always remember that Jesus said, "... and the powers of death shall not prevail against it" (Mt 16: 18). (Also sometimes translated as "the gates of hell" or "the gates of the nether world.") It is only logical that Satan would hate the Church and do his best to destroy it. He will get as many to fall as far away as possible. Jesus knew this, but promised us that the devil would not prevail. There will be sin and corruption, but the Catholic Church will remain.

Given the extent of the corruption in the Church at certain periods of history, if it had been a mere man-made institution, it surely would have crumbled. God promised to protect his Church and he has. The Catholic Church is still the largest Christian denomination, larger than all the others put together, and it continues the traditions and teachings begun by Jesus.

Another very important consideration usually overlooked in any discussion on Church corruption is that Jesus was not only very aware of this sort of corruption, he experienced it firsthand. Jesus chose twelve very human apostles. They sometimes argued, had petty jealousies, ran away when there was trouble; Peter was known for being hotheaded. These were men with flaws and weaknesses, yet Jesus picked them.

So is it surprising that some of our priests and bishops show themselves to be painfully human at times? Even after the Holy Spirit descended upon the apostles, there still were problems and disagreements from time to time. Where there are people, there will be defects and weaknesses. Yet, God left his Church on earth in the hands of mere men—imperfect, sinful men. And who are we to argue with God? He obviously did not expect perfection, but faith in him. Jesus promised to be the way to salvation, and by his choice of twelve apostles he made it clear to us all that salvation is for everyone, flaws and all. It is only human that we fall, but we have the opportunity to keep getting up again through the mercy of Jesus Christ.

In his book *Covenant With Jesus*, Father Robert J. Fox tells us that we should not be overly surprised or upset by the weaknesses of some of our Church leaders. After all, he says, Jesus chose Judas as one of the twelve Apostles. Judas became selfish and greedy and helped himself to the group's money. Little by little he allowed his faith in Jesus and his mission to die, and eventually he betrayed Jesus. What scandal in the Church can top Judas selling the Son of God for thirty pieces of silver? There have been big scandals in our Church's history, but it was one of the chosen apostles, one of Jesus' inner circle, who handed him over to death. So right from the start we see that our faith must be primarily in God and not in people, no matter what their position.

Every organization of people of any size is going to have sinfulness among its members. Every religious body, every Christian denomination, has had serious failures in its members, even in its clergy. I think Jesus, who chose Judas, permitted this among his first priests so that no one could look at the failure of an individual priest or bishop today and condemn the whole Church as a result. Quoting Father Fox: "There was nothing wrong with the seminary Judas attended."

If we attend and belong to a church, our children will accept and expect it to be a part of their lives. They will grow alongside and within a church community rather than on the outside, doing their own thing. Jesus told us we would wither and die without him. By participating in the life of the Church he established, we are sharing in his life.

5

ONE CHURCH

This chapter may seem like a small step from the last one but it is actually a leap in developing a solid faith in the Roman Catholic Church. I am taking you from the idea of recognizing the importance of belonging to an organized church to the idea that the Bible teaches there should be only one Christian church and not the thousands of denominations that exist today.

Once a Christian believes Jesus intended to begin one single Church, he should naturally desire to belong to that Church in order to get closer to God. Jesus and his Church are one. When St. Paul fell to the ground after a light from the sky suddenly flashed about him, he heard a voice saying, " 'Saul, Saul, why do you persecute me?' And he said, 'Who are you, Lord?' And he said, 'I am Jesus, whom you are persecuting; but rise and enter the city, and you will be told what you are to do' " (Acts 9:4–9). Jesus did not ask Saul (later known as Paul, after his baptism) why he was persecuting his *followers*; he asked, "Why do you persecute *me*?"

Many converts to Catholicism believed that Jesus began one church, and they set out to find it. In Patrick Madrid's book *Surprised by Truth*, eleven powerful conversion stories occurred because all eleven people were seeking the one church Christ began. None had considered Catholicism until their search for that one church led them right to it every time they investigated an article of faith. (He has since written two sequels, containing additional testimonies of converts.)

Some of the people I know who do not share a belief in one true church are prone to church shopping. When they are unhappy with a particular church—be it the congregation, the pastor, or just the location—they shop around for another. Church shoppers visit various churches and denominations looking for one that appeals to them. They look for churches the same way they shop for a new car. Sociologists have noted an increasingly consumerist approach to religion in the United States. Issues such as authority, tradition, scriptural interpretation or revelation mean less to church shoppers than the services and outer appearance of the church. It's the look and feel that will ultimately win them over when, instead, it should be the truth. Only if we convince our children that Jesus established a Church and that that Church is the Roman Catholic Church, will we prevent them from becoming future church shoppers.

As Christians, we believe that Jesus Christ is the Son of God, our Savior. There are both similarities and opposing opinions among Christians on what it means to follow Christ. All Christian denominations cannot represent complete truth, because they disagree with one another on many points. As Catholics we believe that our traditions are the traditions begun by Jesus and continued by the apostles and their successors. We believe that we are the one true Church of Jesus Christ.

Older children might sometimes challenge this notion. My own children have asked, "If it is so obvious and so easy to prove, then why isn't everyone Catholic?" The answer is that when people began interpreting Scripture on their own, separate from the Church, different opinions developed, and thus they broke with the one body, the one Church.

In the next chapter we will study the right and authority of the Church to give the correct and authoritative meaning of Scripture and of all parts of Scripture; but I bring it up here to show how interpreting Scripture apart from the Church set Christians on very different courses.

A particular article of faith often hinges on scriptural interpretation. It is easy to get into wrestling matches on minor issues with other denominations, but your children can best anchor their faith on the belief that Jesus established only one true Church. By being firm on the big picture—one church—everything else falls into place. Jesus left one church, not thousands of Christian churches that disagree with one another today.

This point is one you can agree upon with most Christian debaters. Jesus left ONE church. All the non-Catholic Christian religions (aside from the Eastern Orthodox churches) began more than a thousand five hundred years after Jesus ascended into heaven. All these other Christian religions were born of conflict, having a beginning based on an argument or disagreement with scriptural interpretation. Only the Catholic faith can claim its beginnings were with Christ and continued with the apostles and is the very same Church today.

But how can anyone be so sure that out of the thousands of Christian denominations, theirs is the one true faith? One reason is the Roman Catholic Church is united throughout the world as one. The word "Catholic" means "universal" or "all nations." The word of God calls for "one Lord, one faith, one baptism" (Eph 4: 5). Jesus says, "I will build my church" (Mt 16: 18), not churches.

Through the Church God would spread truth:

> That through the church the manifold wisdom of God might be made known to the principalities and powers in the heavenly places. This was according to the eternal purpose which he has realized in Christ Jesus our Lord (Eph 3: 10–11).

Also note that it is through "the church" that God's wisdom will be made known, not through individual Bible reading.

Scripture repeatedly refers to the Church as the "Body of Christ." Today we call the Roman Catholic Church the Mystical Body of Christ; Jesus is the head and we are the members:

> For just as the body is one and has many members, and all the members of the body, though many, are one body, so it is with Christ (1 Cor 12: 12).

> . . . that there may be no discord in the body, but that the members may have the same care for one another (1 Cor 12: 25).

Scripture is very clear that the ideal is to be "one."

> Only let your manner of life be worthy of the gospel of Christ, so that whether I come and see you or am absent, I may hear of you that you stand firm in one spirit, with one mind striving side by side for the faith of the gospel, and not frightened in any thing by your opponents (Phil 1: 27).

> . . . complete my joy by being of the same mind, having the same love, being in full accord and of one mind (Phil 2:2).

The Roman Catholic Church has one head, the pope, and there is one teaching. We can attend Mass in Switzerland or Guatemala or Australia and it is essentially the same Mass. A Catholic Church is a Catholic Church is a Catholic Church. There are some churches that have broken with Rome's directives, but renegade priests and people who call themselves Catholics but don't agree with Church teachings are breaking with Roman Catholicism.

No other Christian religion can make this worldwide claim, as one united body in unison and in agreement on faith and teachings since the apostles. Ever since Martin Luther first splintered the Christian community in 1517, the splintering has continued. Does all this divisiveness matter? We are all Christians, right? Couldn't all the numerous references Jesus made of "one body" and "one church" mean the whole Christian brotherhood? To answer, let me ask you: Is falsehood as good as truth? Could Jesus oppose himself in his teachings? In Luke we read: "But he, knowing their thoughts, said to them, 'Every kingdom divided against itself is laid waste, and house falls upon house' " (Lk 11:17).

Jesus promised that his Church would never be destroyed. So which church is the one true Church? If there is no pure Church that has survived the ages, then Jesus was wrong when he said the gates of hell would not prevail against his Church. This is impossible. Jesus could not have been wrong.

Some people claim that when Christ refers to "one" church, he means it as an invisible church, as in all of Christianity, and not as a particular visible church. But Jesus himself disputes this notion. "You are the light of the world. A city set on a hill cannot be hid" (Mt 5:14).

The word "church" is used more than one hundred times in the New Testament. It is not used once with the meaning of a symbolic, spiritual, or invisible church, or as a plurality of churches. Catholics interpret "church" literally, as an organized group of Jesus' followers united in a common faith, just as it is used each time in the Bible.

"Christ the Lord founded one Church and one Church only," Vatican II tells us clearly, "though many Christian communions present themselves as the true inheritors of Jesus Christ. All indeed profess to be followers of the Lord but they differ in mind and go their different ways, as if Christ himself were divided. Certainly, such division openly contradicts the will of Christ, scandalizes the world, and damages that most holy cause, the preaching of the Gospel to every creature" (*Decree on Ecumenism*, 1). "I beg you," writes St. Paul,

> to lead a life worthy of the calling to which you have been called, . . . eager to maintain the unity of the Spirit in the bond of peace. There is one body and one Spirit, just as you were called to the one hope that belongs to your call, one Lord, one faith, one baptism; one God and Father of us all, who is above all and through all and in all (Eph 4:2–6).

Again and again Scripture speaks of unity and being members of the Body of Christ. Jesus, obviously, wants his children to be united as one family, one Church, embracing the one God, the one truth.

On Holy Thursday, just before Jesus was to be handed over to his death, he prayed and talked to his apostles at length about the importance of unity. He explained that if they did not remain united in one faith, they would hinder the world from believing in him. He said:

> "Holy Father, keep them in thy name, which thou hast given me, that they may be one, even as we are one. While I was with them, I kept them in thy name, which thou hast given me; I have guarded them, and none of them is lost but the son of perdition, that the scripture might be fulfilled. . . . I have given them thy word; and the world has hated them because they are not of the world, even as I am not of the world. . . . Sanctify them in the truth; thy word is truth. As thou didst send me into the world, so I have sent them into the world. And for their sake I consecrate myself, that they also may be consecrated in truth.

"I do not pray for these only, but also for those who believe in me through their word, that they may all may be one; even as thou Father, art in me, and I in thee, that they may also be in us, so that the world may believe that thou hast sent me" (Jn 17:11–21).

St. Paul addressed the importance of unity:

He [Jesus] is before all things, and in him all things hold together. He is the head of the body, the church (Col 1:17–18).

I appeal to you, brethren, by the name of our Lord Jesus Christ, that all of you agree and that there be no dissensions among you, but that you be united in the same mind and the same judgment (1 Cor 1:10).

. . . for the equipment of the saints, for the work of ministry, for building up the body of Christ, until we all attain to the unity of the faith and of the knowledge of the Son of God, to mature manhood, to the measure of the stature of the fulness of Christ (Eph 4:12–13).

Through [him] we have received grace and apostleship to bring about the obedience of the faith for the sake of his name among all the nations, including yourselves who are called to belong to Jesus Christ (Rom 1:5–6).

. . . through the prophetic writings is made known to all nations, according to the command of the eternal God, to bring about the obedience of faith (Rom 16:26).

. . . so we, though many, are one body in Christ, and individually members one of another (Rom 12:5).

. . . complete my joy by being of the same mind, with the same love, being in full accord and of one mind (Phil 2:2).

I appeal to you, brethren, to take note of those who create dissensions and difficulties, in opposition to the doctrine which you have been taught; avoid them" (Rom 16:17).

Reread this last Scripture verse and let the impact of the message sink in. "Avoid" those who create dissensions. In-fighting and divisions preclude the Church being "one" body, so those who create divisions are to be avoided by Church brethren. *Nowhere* in Scripture is the solution to disagreement to split into another denomination.

There are examples of disagreement in the New Testament. For example, chapters 15 and 16 of the Acts of the Apostles. The debate was about whether Gentiles who wanted to become Christian had to embrace the Mosaic Law and be circumcised before they could be baptized and received into the Church. The proper response, as given in Scripture, was to call a council and ponder these questions:

> And when Paul and Barnabas had no small dissension and debate with them, Paul and Barnabas, and some of the others were appointed to go up to Jerusalem to the apostles and the elders about this question (Acts 15:2).

There is no example of splintering. Scripture clearly shows that doctrinal or moral confusion is to be clarified and guidelines are to be issued. The Bible calls for "one" Church with no allowances given for leaving and starting up a new church. The Bible talks about some people who do not accept some aspects of Church teaching and warns them of the seriousness of their errors:

> But these men revile whatever they do not understand, and by those things that they know by instinct as irrational animals do, they are destroyed. Woe to them! For they walk in the way of Cain, and abandon themselves for the sake of gain to Balaam's error, and perish in Korah's rebellion (Jude 10–11).

To understand what the rebellion of Korah was all about, look at Numbers 16. Korah and 250 Israelites held an assembly against Moses and Aaron. They were rebelling against the leadership of Moses and Aaron, wanting to start their own community and establish their own priesthood. Consider what God did to these rebels:

> And as he finished speaking all these words, the ground under them split asunder, and the earth opened its mouth

> and swallowed them up, with their households and all the men that belonged to Korah and all their goods. So they and all that belonged to them went down alive into Sheol; and the earth closed over them, and they perished from the midst of the assembly (Num 16:31–33).

Clearly, rebelling against the Church and authority established by God is not the message preached in the Bible. Although there were heresies and disagreement within the brotherhood of Christians almost from the start, there was still one church. Jesus Christ left one Church and the Catholic Church lays claim to be that same Church, the one true Church. One religious scholar explains the claim as follows:

> The Roman Catholic Church is "one" in Faith and "one" in sacrifice, has one sacramental system, and has one divine head (Christ) and one earthly head (the Pope). The Church is "holy" in her Founder, Jesus Christ, in her teachings, in her means of providing grace (the Sacraments), and in the many members who follow her teachings and use the means of grace She provides.
>
> The Church is "catholic or universal" in that She is the church of all nations and races. The Church is "apostolic" in that She can trace her origin in an unbroken line back to the Apostles on whom Christ founded the Church. No other church possesses all four of these marks.[1]

In spite of our historical claim, anti-Catholic sentiments abound. I have actually been told by non-Catholics that some Christian religions do not even consider Catholics to be Christians. When a new friend of one of my sons came over to play one day and he saw a holy water font in his room, his mouth opened in surprise. "You're Catholic?" he asked.

When my son told him he was, this boy asked, "What if you don't get to heaven?" My son merely replied, "What if you don't?" The kids then proceeded to play nicely for the afternoon, but his mother never let him come over again.

---

[1] Brian Clowes, *Call to Action or Call to Apostacy?* (Front Royal, VA: *Human Life International*, 1977), p. 101.

If your children feel attacked or criticized for being Catholic, remind them that Jesus was also attacked, and we cannot expect better for ourselves.

"A disciple is not above his teacher, nor a servant above his master; it is enough for the disciple to be like his teacher, and the servant like his master. If they have called the master of the house Be-elzebul, how much more will they malign those of his household" (Mt 10: 24).

> "If the world hates you, know that it has hated me before it hated you. If you were of the world, the world would love its own; but because you are not of the world, but I chose you out of the world, therefore the world hates you" (Jn 15: 18–19).

A sign of the Church Jesus left for us is one that is hated by the world for stubbornly refusing to bend to society's changing values. If holding onto Catholic teaching brings us ridicule for being old-fashioned, we can seek comfort in the fact that Jesus told us this would happen.

The Catholic Church is so often seen as "behind the times" and holding women back because women priests are not allowed. The Catholic Church has been accused of holding back entire countries because it resists Planned Parenthood's efforts at full-scale dissemination of artificial birth control methods. It is worth noting that all Christian denominations were once against artificial birth control up until the 1930s. When society's values began changing, one by one the other churches changed their teaching. Some denominations changed so completely that now they actually promote artificial birth control. The Catholic Church alone stands firm, its teaching unchanged since apostolic times.

One of my children once asked, "Why do other Christian religions criticize Catholics so often?" I explained that when a group breaks away from another, there is usually disagreement. Since the Catholic faith is the same "one" Church, it has never broken away from another. Other religions feel the need to justify themselves. They give reasons why they broke away from the Catholic faith and often these come in the form of criticism and attacks. The same goes for persecution within the Church. Those who turn their backs on Church teaching often criticize those who continue to embrace that teaching.

Our children need to anticipate criticism of their Catholic faith as they go through life, so it does not upset them. Acknowledge that their feelings might even get hurt sometimes, but certainly Jesus had sad feelings when people rejected the truth he was bringing them.

The Catholic Church has the fullness of truth and all the means of holiness. The Protestant churches—or ecclesial communities, as they are more correctly called—have many elements of the truth and some of the means of holiness. They have only two of the sacraments, Baptism and matrimony. They do not have the other five sacraments since they do not have the ministerial priesthood. We want all non-Catholics to come to know our church, to recognize that she is the one true Church, founded by Christ, and to have the grace to convert and become Catholic, under the Pope. Each year from January 18 to 25, we celebrate Church Unity Week, during which we pray for that intention.

Pope John Paul II was very committed to ecumenism. "The Catholic Church, I can affirm, is committed at every level to frank ecumenical dialogue, without facile optimism but also without distrust or without hesitation or delays," he said in the Apostolic Exhortation *On Reconciliation and Penance* (no. 25). When talking to our separated brethren about these matters "we should do so with love for the truth, with charity and with humility" (Vatican II, *Decree on Ecumenism*, no. 11).

Pope Benedict XVI, in the homily at his first Mass after becoming Pope, said:

> I assume as my primary commitment that of working tirelessly towards the reconstitution of the full and visible unity of all Christ's followers. This is my ambition, this is my compelling duty. I am aware that to do so, expressions of good feelings are not enough. Concrete gestures are required to penetrate souls and move consciences, encouraging everyone to that interior conversion which is the basis for all progress on the road of ecumenism.

So, as we thank God for our faith and for the Catholic Church, we encourage our children to be grateful to God and to be proud to be Catholic. When they form friendships with other Christians they should be courteous and respectful of their religious beliefs, and happy to explain the Catholic faith to anyone with questions.

6

CHURCH AUTHORITY

If we accept that Jesus began one church—the Roman Catholic Church—then recognizing that God speaks to us through that Church is the next logical step. To follow Christ fully, we need to follow those he put in charge in his Church: "he who listens to you listens to me," Christ said to the apostles, and to their successors, the pope and the bishops.

Since we cannot prepare our children for every argument against Catholicism, we teach them to have trust and confidence in the pope and the teaching authority of the Catholic Church. If we accomplish this, everything else will fall into place. Questions and issues will not drive them away, because they will remember that Christ—just before his ascension into heaven—said to his apostles: "All authority in heaven and earth has been given to me. Go therefore and make disciples of all nations, baptizing them in the name of the Father and of the Son and of the Holy Spirit, teaching them to observe all that I have commanded you; and lo, I am with you always, to the close of the age" (Mt 28:18–20). Christ is with his Church at all times and we know that we can always rely on the Church's teaching. With such faith, being at a loss for an answer or hearing of some scandal within the Church need not become stumbling blocks for them.

Most denominational differences boil down to one question—whose authority do you follow? Your own? Martin Luther's? A favorite preacher's? Or the word of God that comes to us through the Catholic Church? Putting ourselves under the authority of another is not the way of the world these days. Accepting that Christ speaks to us through the teaching of the Catholic Church in all matters to do with faith and morals is even considered rather extreme by some Catholics today.

Some of you might think, "I don't agree with the Church on everything!" If that's the case, you are not alone. Many Catholics have their own ideas about birth control, abortion, whether women should be in the priesthood, unisex unions, and so on. But remember, there can only be one teaching of Jesus Christ. He cannot contradict himself. If you have an opinion different from the Catholic Church's on a matter of faith or morals, you cannot both be right. So who has the authority to make these judgments? Whom did Jesus promise to lead in truth with the Holy Spirit: his Church or individuals?

If you do not accept Church authority or some aspect of it, then you are not accepting a fundamental Church teaching. If this is the case, then you cannot possibly hand down a strong faith in the Church to your children. You will have already watered it down. If you are in error, you are teaching your children error. You cannot hand down most of the faith and then disagree on a few items. In that case, you will have already taught them it is okay to hold opinions opposing Catholic teaching. As one of our parish priests once said, "Either you believe in everything Jesus taught, or you believe in none of it." At first I thought these were pretty harsh words, but think about it. If Jesus tells us to be obedient and follow his teachings and we don't, we are not truly following him.

Maybe I have not convinced you. Throughout this chapter I will show why it is so important to accept Catholic Church authority. If you disregard this authority and pick and choose what you want to believe, you are no different from the groups that broke away because they had their own ideas. The choice is between Catholicism's authority or our own interpretation, or someone else's interpretation, of what God wants us to know and follow.

We accept and embrace what Jesus Christ reveals to us and what the Church teaches us not because we understand or agree with it, but because of the authority of God who reveals and teaches those truths, and God can never deceive nor be deceived, as Vatican Council I tells us.

We should be continually learning more about God and his Church, reading the Old and New Testaments, and books about the history of the Church from the first centuries to our time. We should read the writings of the Fathers of the Church, the saints, the Popes, and the *Catechism of the Catholic Church*. There is so much to learn and know. And we should always listen to the

Pope, the magisterium of the Church, and the bishops. Listen to them and heed what they say. Only the Pope is infallible. The Holy Spirit preserves him from error when he teaches in matters of faith and morals and states that it is to be held by all the faithful. In that case the Holy Spirit guarantees that he is correct in what he teaches.

> . . . if I am delayed, you may know how one ought to behave in the household of God, which is the church of the living God, the pillar and bulwark of truth (1 Tim 3: 15).

We should follow the indications of our conscience when it is properly formed; in other words, when we have a good knowledge of Jesus Christ and his teachings and the teachings of his Church. Conscience is like a referee in a game of football or basketball. A good referee doesn't make up or change the rules of the sport in question. He is a good referee insofar as he has a good knowledge of the rules and applies them to the actions of the players, deciding whether a particular action was fair (acceptable) or unfair (a foul). In the moral order, the commandments of God and the precepts of the Church constitute the book of rules, or the supreme norms of morality and right living. The task of conscience is to know those norms, to apply them to our actions and to decide whether or not our actions are good or bad, whether they are pleasing to God or not. God seeks our eternal happiness, and he knows best how we can attain it. Therefore, we need to seek his authority, which we can find in his Church. Consider the following explanation:

Those who embrace the supremacy of human conscience by definition discard objective truth, because the unfettered "conscience" is notoriously flexible, compromising and rationalizing when temptation strikes.

Dissenters are very fond of quoting the Vatican II document *Dignitatis Humanae* (Declaration on Religious Freedom), in support of their contention that we should be able to do anything our "conscience" does not object to. However, Father John Courtney Murray, S.J., principal author of the Declaration, anticipated this kind of dishonesty. He stated, in a footnote to the Abbott-Gallagher edition of the Council texts:

> The Declaration does not base the right to the free exercise of religion on "freedom of conscience." Nowhere does this phrase occur. And the Declaration nowhere lends its authority to the theory for which the phrase frequently stands, namely, that I have the right to do what my conscience tells me to do, simply because my conscience tells me to do it. This is a perilous theory. Its particular peril is subjectivism—the notion that, in the end, it is my conscience, and not the objective truth, which determines what is right and wrong, true or false.[1]

There are many who say the Church is simply too out-of-date to direct our lives. Apparently, they think Jesus should have put an expiration date on some of his teachings. The problem with this argument is that if Jesus is God, he could have looked ahead and realized times would change. He could have addressed his teachings as conditional. He did not do this. If Jesus is right, sin during the first century is sin in the twenty-first century. He simply did not mention societal changes as a reason to engage in behaviors that he originally taught were sinful.

Looking to the Church's authority rather than our own opinions or personal scriptural interpretations sets us apart from other Christian denominations but it is exactly what the first Christians did. Early Christian writings confirm that the Church honored three ways to follow our faith. One is belief in the Bible. The second is following tradition with a capital T—God's authority not man's. The third is obeying the authority Christ gave us in his Church, the "magisterium"—the teaching of the Pope and bishops acting in unity.

Let's consider the first way—belief in the Bible as our guide. Catholics accept the Bible as our guide, but not over and above the Church. Many denominations have an historically recent tradition of *sola scriptura*. This is a phrase coined during the 1500's when Protestant Reformers broke with the Catholic Church. It rejects tradition and Church authority through her leaders and claims that Scripture teaches everything we need to know about

---

[1] W. M. Abbott, ed., *The Documents of Vatican II* (New York: America Press, 1966), p. 679.

Christ and his Church. *Sola scriptura* claims the Bible and the Bible alone is our authority. And if it is not in the Bible, it doesn't count for anything.

Jesus' teachings were recorded in the Bible thanks to the Catholic Church. The Church is responsible for the Bible, not the other way around. Jesus did not write a book. Jesus spoke to his disciples, he did not write things down. When he ascended into heaven there was no book. Jesus left a Church built upon the apostles, who were guided by the Holy Spirit and given authority to teach in his name. The New Testament came some years later, and it was only at the end of the fourth century that the Church compiled an official list or "canon" of the books that were universally accepted as inspired. Here is a brief explanation of this history:

> The canon of the Bible as we have it today was accepted by the Church Council of Hippo (A.D. 393) and its decisions were reaffirmed by the two councils of Carthage in 397 and 419. The same canon of the Bible has been reaffirmed repeatedly by Popes and councils throughout the centuries. The Ecumenical Council of Trent, on April 8, 1546, which took place shortly after the Protestant Revolt, formally and dogmatically canonized these books, numbering 45 of the Old Testament and 27 of the New Testament. Unless there was such an authority of the Church speaking in the name of Jesus Christ, we would have no way of knowing which writings were authentically inspired and which were falsely claimed to be inspired.[2]

The Protestant tradition of *sola scriptura* is not only not scriptural but it is based on the fact that the Catholic Church made infallible decisions in selecting sacred, infallible books for the New Testament. At the same time that Protestants adopted the belief of *sola scriptura*, they threw out some of the books of the Bible as uninspired. Some 1500 hundred years after the New Testament was compiled, Protestants took a book they agreed was infallible and divinely inspired and declared parts

[2] Fr. Robert Fox, *Covenant with Jesus* (South Dakota: Fatima Family Apostolate, 1996), p. 80.

of it uninspired. The rest—the parts they determined should remain—they consider not only infallible, but the only source of truth. This is inconsistent and unbiblical:

> Since the Bible does not indicate which books belong within it, and since Protestants do not believe the Church has any authority to infallibly determine which books belong and which books don't, Protestants are left in an epistemological dilemma. Hence they are forced to the logical but heretical conclusion that there may be inspired books that should be in the Bible but were left out in error, and that there may be uninspired books in the Bible that have no business being there, but were added in error.
>
> Martin Luther, for example, wanted to delete the books of James, Hebrews 2, Peter, and Revelation, since he believed they were added in error. If it had not been for the persuasion of his contemporaries, these books may well have been deleted from Protestant Bibles.
>
> In holding to the "fallible canon" theory, Protestants cannot be infallibly certain that the Bible they hold in their hands is in fact the Bible. The issue of the canon is an unsolvable epistemological problem for Protestants. For if one cannot be certain which books belong in the Bible, how can one presume to use it "alone" as a reliable guide to saving faith in God? The irony is that while Protestants use the theory of *sola scriptura* to advance their attacks on the Catholic Church, they have no infallible way of knowing what comprises Scripture in the first place.[3]

Nowhere does the Bible state that Scripture is the sole rule of faith. Passages from John and Timothy are often used to defend *sola scriptura*, so let's take a look at them:

(*a*) "Search the scriptures . . ." (Jn 5:39). Here, Jesus was rebuking disbelieving Jews, and telling them the Old Testament

---

[3] Bob Sungenis, in Patrick Madrid, *Surprised by Truth* (San Diego: Basilica Press, 1994), pp. 123–124.

prophesies were fulfilled in him. He was not saying the Bible was the sole authority.

(*b*) "All scripture is inspired by God and profitable for teaching, for reproof, for correction, and for training in righteousness, that the man of God may be complete, equipped for every good work" (2 Tim 3:16–17). Even though the book of Timothy goes on to hold Scripture in high esteem, it is clearly a tool, not the be-all and end-all. Paul, in instructing Timothy, gives high praise to Scripture, just as the Catholic Church does. He tells him to hold fast to the doctrine that has been handed down to him. Paul then says Scripture is divinely inspired and has various uses. But this passage does not say only Scripture. If the message *was* only Scripture then saying it "is profitable for teaching . . ." would not convey the correct message. Something that is the only authority would not be referred to as being "profitable for teaching," but rather it would need to be called the singular—the one and only—source for instruction.

Keep in mind that the Scripture Paul is referring to is the Old Testament. The New Testament did not exist as a canon of the Bible at that time. So if Paul were instructing Timothy to follow *only* Scripture, that it was all sufficient, then he was telling Timothy that the Old Testament was all he needed. We know that the Bible without the New Testament is not a sufficient rule of faith for Christians. Further:

> Look at the words carefully. There is no mention about Scripture being sufficient, on its own. Paul says Scripture is "profitable" for these various ends. That doesn't mean some other thing, or other things, might not be profitable also. Consider an analogy. We might say that water is profitable for bodily health—that it can help us achieve it—but that isn't the same thing as saying water is all we need to remain healthy. We need solid food and exercise too. Paul says Scripture is profitable, but he doesn't say it's the only thing that is profitable. Profitableness doesn't equal sufficiency.[4]

[4] Karl Keating, *The Usual Suspects* (San Francisco: Ignatius Press, 2000), p. 52.

Scripture without the Church is writing without authority behind it. That would be like setting up rules for a corporation without an administrator, or writing the Constitution of the United States but not allocating governing and interpreting branches of government. If all the United States had were a written document, interpretations would (and do) abound, but there would be no body or bodies to interpret officially. Our founding fathers knew as much, so would God inspire writings without providing a living authority to interpret and guide? Denominations that rejected the Church left themselves with only the Bible as their sole guide. This is not as Jesus left it. There was no Christian Bible for many years after Jesus ascended into heaven. Did this mean there was no authority? How can a book, a nonliving object that did not even exist for years after Christianity began, be the sole authority? A book cannot interpret itself and nowhere in the Bible does it state that the Bible is the sole authority. This would imply that Jesus taught for three years, then left nothing to guide his infant Church until years later when the Bible was finally completed. Yet, during the time between Christ's ascension and the definitive canon of the New Testament, the Church experienced a tremendous period of growth—all through word of mouth.

The Church came first and the New Testament followed. It is a guide but it is not above the Church. It was the world's oldest and largest religious body, the Catholic Church, that compiled and preserved the Bible for all of Christianity. It was the only Christian denomination with a single version of the Bible until the sixteenth century. Anyone who declares "only" the Bible has the truth is admitting that the Catholic Church made an infallible decision hundreds of years after the last apostle died. The nonexistent Bible could not tell anyone which writings were divinely inspired and belonged in the Bible. It was the Catholic Church, with God-given authority, that was guided to discern infallibly which were the sacred writings.

Prior to the Reformation, the principle of sola scriptura is not found in early Christian writings with the exception of a few writers not connected to each other and not holding otherwise Protestant views. The writings of the early Church Fathers support the belief that traditions and Church authority are important in handing down religion. The Catholic position that Scripture is important but not "all sufficient" is supported by Scripture itself:

> First of all you must understand this, that no prophecy of scripture is a matter of one's own interpretation, for no prophecy ever came by the impulse of man, but men moved by the Holy Spirit spoke from God (2 Pet 1:20–21).

> And count the forbearance of our Lord as salvation. So also our beloved brother Paul wrote to you according to the wisdom given him, speaking of this as he does in all his letters. There are some things in him hard to understand, which the ignorant and unstable twist to their own destruction, as they do the other scriptures (2 Pet 3:15–16).

How can private interpretation preserve the teachings of Jesus when so many interpretations abound? The Bible represents historical writings compiled and translated from more than one language. The average layman is not going to understand and appreciate all the subtleties:

> So Philip ran to him, and heard him reading Isaiah the prophet, and asked, "Do you understand what you are reading?" And he said, "How can I, unless someone guides me?" (Acts 8:30–31).

The Catholic interpretation of Scripture is based on tradition, knowledge of the geographic and cultural region, original language it was written in, and historical teaching. But most of all, Catholic teaching is based on the guidance of the Holy Spirit and Jesus' promise to keep his Church in truth and the authority he gave to his Church. Jesus directed people to be guided by a living authority. There is nothing in divine revelation that says you have the ability to interpret the Bible without error, according to the mind of Jesus Christ. There is, however, much in the Bible to tell you to listen to the Church, whether by tradition or sacred Scripture and you will be hearing Jesus Christ.

This brings us to sacred Tradition. Scripture is a big part of Tradition but it is only one part. *Sola scriptura* excludes Tradition as a source for identifying and defining religious teaching.

The "Bible only" theory creates a very narrow perspective. Not only does it limit the development of a Church but it ignores history, saints, the writings of the early Church Fathers, and the customs that made Christianity attractive to a largely pagan world.

Tradition tells us how the Church evolved after the death of the last apostle, what happened to Mary, the Mother of Christ, and how Peter and Paul ended their lives. It is Tradition that tells us how early Christian worship developed into the Mass as it exists today and how the Church applied revelation to the everyday needs of the growing congregations. The New Testament does not tell us about the great martyrs, saints, and evangelists, whose heroic self-sacrifice built up the Church in the early centuries and beyond. The writings of the early Church Fathers, instructed by the apostles themselves, go largely ignored by *sola scriptura* followers. Yet, these men who developed Christian thought, and recorded it for ages to come, give written testimony of the early Church. The New Testament offers a glimpse of early Christianity but sacred Tradition fills in the holes. To receive the total revelation of the Church, we cannot ignore Tradition. The Bible even tells us so.

Attacks are often made on Catholics, claiming that Jesus did not tell us to follow Tradition, but actually condemned it. This quote from Scripture is often used to criticize following Catholic Tradition: "You leave the commandment of God, and hold fast the tradition of men." He went on to say, "You have a fine way of rejecting the commandment of God, in order to keep your tradition!" (Mk 7:8–9).

We need to understand that traditions of man are not the same as those of God's authority. In the passage above, Jesus was admonishing the Pharisees for corrupt human traditions that undermine God's divine Tradition. The Pharisees criticized the apostles for eating without washing their hands as prescribed by Jewish tradition. They considered themselves superior for following tradition, but, in reality, they were lacking in love and were not serving God by their attacks. Quoting Isaiah, Jesus said, " . . . This people honors me with their lips, but their hearts are far from me; in vain do they worship me, teaching as doctrines the precepts of men" (Mk 7:6–7).

Jesus actually told us to follow sacred tradition, that makes it a divine command from God. The tradition of *sola scriptura* is a more recent one of man's doing. No writings of the early Church Fathers express a belief that only Scripture can be relied on. This belief did not exist until well over a thousand years after the New Testament was accepted. If you read Scripture in light of this historical fact, the tradition of *sola scriptura* is one that disregards God's command, to uphold instead man's tradition (Mark 7:8-9).

> So then, brethren, stand firm and hold to the traditions which you were taught by us, either by word of mouth or by letter (2 Thess 2: 15).

> Now we command you, brethren, in the name of our Lord Jesus Christ, that you keep away from any brother who is living in idleness and not in accord with the tradition that you received from us (2 Thess 3: 6).

Jesus strongly upheld following divine tradition. The scribes and Pharisees were bad examples but Jesus still told his followers to follow the tradition they laid out for them:

> Then Jesus said to the crowds and to his disciples, "The scribes and the Pharisees sit on Moses' seat; so practice and observe whatever they tell you, but not what they do; for they preach, but do not practice" (Mt 23: 1–3).

Catholics hold to sacred tradition, the very same tradition adhered to by early Christians. Sacred tradition and the Bible never oppose one another unless a nontraditional interpretation of Scripture outside the Church is being used.

Some of the tradition passed on through apostolic teachings includes infant baptism, the Trinity, the true presence of Jesus in the Eucharist, the inerrancy of the Bible, Mary's perpetual virginity and Assumption into heaven, and purgatory. Some things we learn through tradition are not spelled out explicitly in the Bible, although much of Scripture supports these teachings, and nowhere does it contradict them. (Sacred tradition should not be confused with customs such as not eating meat on Fridays or praying the rosary.)

We have covered the first two ways early Christians recognized the Church's authority—through tradition and Scripture. The third and final way was by recognizing Church leaders as God's divine representatives and accepting their teachings and decisions.

Jesus founded a living Church:

> And Jesus came up and said to them, "All authority in heaven and earth has been given to me. Go therefore and make disciples of all nations, baptizing them in the name of the Father and of the Son and of the Holy Spirit, teaching them to observe all that I have commanded you; and lo, I am with you always, to the close of the age" (Mt 28: 18–20).
>
> As the Father has sent me, even so I send you (Jn 20: 21).

It was the apostles whom he told to go out and teach all nations. They had teaching authority. Jesus did not tell them to go and write a book. This came later. By this fact alone, the primacy and authority of the Church is established right from the beginning.

> Obey your leaders and submit to them; for they are keeping watch over your souls, as men who will have to give an account . . . (Heb 13: 17).
>
> . . . what you have heard from me before many witnesses entrust to faithful men who will be able to teach others also (2 Tim 2: 2).
>
> They devoted themselves to the apostles' teaching . . . (Acts 2: 42).

Jesus taught us to go to the Church for instruction. This includes our need for instruction regarding all matters pertaining to our salvation. For instance, he told us to correct our brother who sins against us. If the offender does not listen, then we are to go to him with one or two others to confront the sin objectively.

> If he refuses to listen to them, tell it to the church; and if he refuses to listen even to the church, let him be to you as a Gentile or a tax collector. Truly, I say to you, what-

> ever you bind on earth shall be bound in heaven, and whatever you loose on earth shall be loosed in heaven (Mt 18:17–18).

Go to Acts 15:1–21. Even before all the apostles died, we have the first recorded Church Council, the Council of Jerusalem. This council was convened to determine whether the Mosaic law was necessary for salvation. The Church leaders needed to make this call. Peter and James spoke and explained the council's conclusion. There is no reference to checking with Scripture or any written instructions. The determination of this religious matter rested on the decision of the Church's leaders.

The passage below is from a former Protestant who was determined to find a Protestant version of the early Church. Instead, he kept finding confirmation of the tradition of Catholic Church authority through her leaders:

> The writings of the Church Fathers clearly show that the early Church was Catholic long before the time of the Emperor Constantine. St. Ignatius, bishop of Antioch who knew St. John and who wrote in A.D. 110, speaks of the Church of Rome having primacy. He said the Roman Church has "the presidency of love." A shiver went up my spine when I read these words from Ignatius: "Let no man do aught of things pertaining to the Church apart from the bishop. Let that be held a valid Eucharist which is under the bishop or one to whom he shall have committed it. Wheresoever the bishop shall appear, there let the people be; even as where Jesus may be, there is the Catholic Church.[5]

Jesus gave his apostles, the leaders of his Church, authority, with supreme authority given to Peter. Our pope and bishops of today can trace their power back to Peter and the original apostles. This unbroken chain—apostolic succession—is the very authority of the Roman Catholic Church:

> "And I tell you, you are Peter, and on this rock I will build my church, and the powers of death shall not prevail against it. I will give you the keys of the kingdom of

[5] Patrick Madrid, *Surprised by Truth*, testimony by Tim Staples, pp. 236–237.

> heaven, and whatever you bind on earth shall be bound in heaven, and whatever you loose on earth shall be loosed in heaven" (Mt 16: 18–19).
>
> "Truly, I say to you, whatever you bind on earth shall be bound in heaven, and whatever you loose on earth shall be loosed in heaven" (Mt 18: 18).

Christ did not give us, as individuals, the power to bind and loose. He gave that power to the leaders of his Church. The Bible tells us that Jesus would have more to tell us than what he revealed while he walked on earth. That alone is evidence that everything is not contained in the Bible.

"I have yet many things to say to you, but you cannot bear them now. But when the Spirit of truth comes, he will guide you into all the truth" (Jn 16: 12–13). If the Spirit were giving his messages on "all the truth" to every individual, the result would not be thousands of denominations going in different directions. He speaks through his Church.

During the Last Supper, Jesus spoke of the Holy Spirit—the Advocate—who would keep the Church united in truth:

> "When the Spirit of truth comes, he will guide you into all the truth; for he will not speak on his own authority, but whatever he hears he will speak, and he will declare to you the things that are to come. He will glorify me, for he will take what is mine and declare it to you" (Jn 16: 13–14).

Some say that Jesus had his apostles but that is where the official Church ended—no apostolic succession. This is irrational since it would not be possible to teach all nations in their lifetime and why would Jesus establish an organization only to have it fold within a few years, with the death of the apostles? Shortly after Jesus ascended into heaven, the apostles gathered to choose another to replace Judas. Either they had the authority given by Christ to do this, or the Church was in error right from the start. Scripture repeatedly supports that the apostles had authority. They were the beginning Church—Christ's representatives:

> So then the Lord Jesus, after he had spoken to them, was taken up into heaven, and sat down at the right hand of

> God. And they went forth and preached everywhere, while the Lord worked with them and confirmed the message by the signs that attended it (Mk 16: 19–20).
>
> "And if any one will not receive you or listen to your words, shake off the dust from your feet as you leave that house or town. Truly, I say to you, it shall be more tolerable on the day of judgment for the land of Sodom and Gomorrah than for that town" (Mt 10: 14–15).
>
> "He who hears you hears me, and he who rejects you, rejects me, and he who rejects me rejects him who sent me" (Lk 10: 16).
>
> "And I will pray the Father, and he will give you another Counselor, to be with you for ever, even the Spirit of truth, whom the world cannot receive, because it neither sees him nor knows him; you know him, for he dwells with you, and will be in you. I will not leave you desolate; I will come to you" (Jn 14: 16–18).

In Timothy, the importance and authority of the Church as a living, teaching body, are emphasized: ". . . and what you have heard from me before many witnesses entrust to faithful men who will be able to teach others also" (2 Tim 2: 2).

Jesus gave his apostles his own authority and he promised to send the Holy Spirit to keep them in truth, and he assured them that the gates of hell would never prevail against his Church. He was speaking to ordinary men at the time and not writing down instructions in a book. Christ's Church began with the authority he handed down. Authority through entrusted leaders and tradition came first, and scripture followed later, thanks to that authority. If the Catholic Church fell into error, then Jesus did not keep his word. This is *not* possible. This leaves us with only one conclusion: the Catholic Church cannot be in error.

> Teach and urge these duties. if any one teaches otherwise and does not agree with the sound words of our Lord Jesus Christ and the teaching which accords with godliness, he is puffed up with conceit, he knows nothing; he

has a morbid craving for controversy and for disputes about words (1 Tim 6:3).

Among those who claim the Catholic Church fell into error, some say they refuse to accept the authority of Church leaders in a Church in which there has been sin and corruption. Such a Church, they insist, cannot speak with God's authority. People may even point to some current scandal involving the Church. But consider, that in spite of scandals, and in spite of constant opposition from the world during its nearly two thousand years of existence, the Catholic Church continues to stand strong.

Any merely human organization (with such members) would have collapsed centuries ago. Yet the Catholic Church is today the most vigorous Christian church in the world (and the largest, with over a billion members: more than one-sixth of the human race). That is testimony not to the shrewdness of the Church's leaders, but to the protection of the Holy Spirit.

The Church is a living institution made up of human beings, all prone to sin. In every age the Church has had to endure rebellion, heresy, and scandal among its members. Teaching without error is not the same as teaching without sin. (Infallibility is explained in the chapter on the pope). All the members of the human race are sinners and that includes all the members of the Catholic Church and all other churches and religions. Church leaders are also sinners, who struggle to be saints. After all, Jesus began his Church knowingly with one of the most notorious of sinners, Judas. His Church was built on truth, but that truth existed through the power and protection of God in spite of any sinfulness on the part of Church members. He selected Judas to be an apostle. Was he showing us not to give up on his Church because of any man's sin? There was sin during Jesus' time on earth, and there will, unfortunately, be sin on earth until the end of time.

If you care to look further, the following texts also support accepting the Church as a living teacher and following her traditions: Acts 2:42; Col 2:22; 2 Cor 10:8; 1 Cor 11:2; Eph 3:4–11; Eph 2:20; Eph 4:21; Jn 14:16; Lk 10:16; 2 Thess 2:15; 2 Tim 2:2.

To belong to a church truly, we must have faith in that

church. To be unsure of some aspect of Church teaching usually means that we lack information or understanding. So, we need to seek advice or guidance, and to read or study, and ask the Holy Spirit to enlighten and help us.. To have complete faith in our religion, we must be able to look to an infallible church, one protected from teaching in error. It would be unwise to trust our soul to a church that could not claim infallibility. I want my children to believe and trust in the Roman Catholic Church. If we reject the Church's authority, then we are rejecting the Church, and if we reject the Church we are, to a large extent, rejecting Christ.

Although this has been a long lesson, we can summarize it for children quite simply. The Catholic Church's teachings are based on the traditions of the early Christians, on Scripture, which is a part of that tradition, and on the authority Jesus gave his Church's leaders. When opportunities present themselves to get into deeper discussions regarding Church authority with your children, you can use scriptural passages to support your teaching.

I have written at some length about Church authority because it is crucial that you, the parent, are convinced of the Church's rightful authority if you hope to raise your children as strong Catholics. And, secondly, I believe that when we accept the authority of the Catholic Church, everything else falls into place. Even if we fail to understand the reasons for our Church's teachings, the fact that we accept them because we accept her authority will keep us on track.

Of course I am not suggesting we not bother with the rest. The more we know about our Catholic faith, the greater our ability to embrace and share it with others. But it is that core belief, that the Catholic Church speaks with God's authority, that will be our base.

7

THE POPE

In accepting that the Roman Catholic Church has God-given authority in our lives, we must acknowledge the pope as the head of the Church. The pope is the divinely appointed vicar (substitute) of Christ. For many, looking to a mere man—the pope—for leadership is another stumbling block to embracing the Roman Catholic faith fully.

If Catholic teaching is correct, then the pope is the vicar of Christ, and if we ignore his authority then we ignore God himself. If God truly gave the pope his authority on earth, then to disregard his teachings puts our soul in serious danger. So, we must instill in the hearts and minds of our children the fact that the pope is Christ's representative and the head of his Church here on earth.

> Let every person be subject to the governing authorities. For there is no authority except from God, and those that exist have been instituted by God. Therefore he who resists the authorities resists what God has appointed, and those who resist will incur judgment (Rom 13: 1–2).

You can explain to young children that the pope is the head of the Roman Catholic Church here on earth, the successor to St. Peter as Bishop of Rome, and acts in the place of Jesus. Jesus is still head of his body, the Church. (Early Christian writings show that from the earliest times, the bishop of Rome has been called "pope"—*papa*, in Latin and in Italian.)

Jesus promised to keep his Church in truth. So whenever the pope makes known he is teaching officially from the Chair [of Authority] (known as *ex cathedra*) on issues of faith or morals, he is being kept free from error. When the pope makes a solemn pronouncement *ex cathedra*, his teaching is free from error.

It is important to point out that official teaching is not the same as devotional practices and man-made traditions. Some people accuse the Catholic Church of changing her laws and regulations. "Catholics used to say it was a sin to eat meat on Friday and now your Church says it's all right," some argue. Not eating meat on Friday was a regulation made by the Church encouraging people to make a sacrifice on Friday in honor of Christ's crucifixion on Good Friday. After Vatican II, the Church held on to the practice of making a sacrifice on Fridays, but decided to leave it up to each individual what that sacrifice would be.

Children should understand that Jesus put the pope in charge and that we can trust his leadership. Since attacks on the pope can be nasty (at times he is even accused of being the antichrist), older children need to deepen their understanding and appreciation of the pope's leadership. The more they read Scripture and the history of the Church and the popes, the more they'll see the loving hand of God guiding the Church.

Jesus established his Church with a leader, beginning with Peter. Peter's original name was Simon. Jesus changed his name from Simon to Cephas, which has come to us through the Greek (*Petros*) as "Peter." Cephas means rock in Aramaic, which is the language Jesus spoke. "So you are Simon the son of John? You shall be called Cephas" (Jn 1:42). In Aramaic, *Cephas*, as used by Jesus, meant a large rock. (Some translations use the word *Kephas*, which is another spelling.)

Everything Jesus did had a purpose. Eventually Jesus made his purpose known. "'And I tell you, you are Peter, and on this rock I will build my church, and the powers of death shall not prevail against it. I will give you the keys of the kingdom of heaven, and whatever you bind on earth shall be bound in heaven, and whatever you loose on earth shall be loosed in heaven'" (Mt 16:18–19).

It is interesting to note that, in the Old Testament, God was called rock, but also Abraham is referred to as the rock from which the Old Covenant people of God were hewn.

> Hearken to me, you who pursue deliverance,
> you who seek the LORD;
> look to the rock from which you were hewn,
> and to the quarry from which you were digged.

> Look to Abraham your father
> and to Sarah who bore you;
> for when he was but one I called him,
> and I blessed him and made him many.
>
> —Is 51:1–2

Abraham was the father of the Old Covenant people—Israel—and Peter became the patriarch of the New Covenant people—Christianity. Just as God chose Abraham in the Old Testament, he chose Peter to lead his people in the New Testament.

Some Protestants argue against the scriptural interpretation of Peter being the rock upon which Christ built his Church on the grounds that in the Greek text the name for Peter is *Petros*, a masculine noun, whereas rock is a feminine noun, *petra*. The Greek translator could use *petra* in the second translation of "upon this rock I built my church," but since Peter was male, it would be inappropriate to give a man a feminine name. So a masculine ending was put on it for Peter—*Petros.*

This difference in noun endings gives rise to debate because the Greek *petros* is commonly used as a small, movable stone. *Petra* means a solid, fixed rock. Using these different word-meanings, detractors maintain that Peter was not intended to be the rock on which Christ built his Church. Some say that, according to the Greek translation, the rock in the second part of the sentence—*petros*, meaning small stone—is emphasizing Peter's insignificance. According to that interpretation, Christ is telling Peter he is but a mere stone, but he will build his Church on the Rock (the large rock), which is the revelation that Jesus is Christ, the Savior.

Look closely at what is actually being said in Matthew 16:17–19:

> Jesus answered him, "Blessed are you, Simon Bar-Jona! For flesh and blood has not revealed this to you, but my Father who is in heaven. And I tell you, you are Peter, and on this rock I will build my church, and the powers of death shall not prevail against it. I will give you the keys of the kingdom of heaven, and whatever you bind on earth shall be bound in heaven, and whatever you loose on earth shall be loosed in heaven."

In this passage Peter is promised primacy over the whole church, a primacy which Jesus confers on him after his resurrection: see John 21:15–18.. Notice that Jesus individually gave Peter the power to bind and loose first and then later gave the same power to the apostles as a group. It was only to Peter, however, that Jesus gave the keys to the kingdom of heaven. In the same breath, would he be calling Peter an insignificant little pebble, but here are the keys to my kingdom anyway?

> . . . the Lord's three statements to Peter had two parts, and the second parts explain the first. The reason Peter was "blessed" was because "flesh and blood has not revealed this to you, but my Father who is in heaven" (v. 17). The meaning of the name change, "You are Rock," is explained by the promise, "On this rock I will build my church, and the powers of death shall not prevail against it" (v. 18). The purpose of the keys is explained by Jesus' commission, "Whatever you bind on earth shall be bound in heaven, and whatever you loose on earth shall be loosed in heaven" (v. 19). A careful reading of these three statements, paying attention to their immediate context and interrelatedness, clearly shows that Peter was the rock about which Jesus spoke.[1]

This whole big rock/little rock argument might seem a bit too complicated to get into with young children. They need to be old enough to understand that some languages have different endings for feminine and masculine nouns. This issue of Jesus' meaning behind calling Peter "rock" would likely only come up for an older child. The quickest way to put it in perspective is to say, "It's all Greek to me, and so what? Jesus did not speak Greek to his disciples."

Christ spoke Aramaic, the common language of Palestine during that time. Matthew's Gospel was originally written in Aramaic before getting translated into Greek. In Aramaic, the word for rock is *cepha*, and there is no translation problem with it. *Cepha* has the same ending whether it refers to a rock or is used as a man's name.

---

[1] James Akin, in Patrick Madrid, *Surprised by Truth* (San Diego: Basilica Press, 1994), p. 69.

Another argument commonly used against Peter as head of Christ's Church on earth is that Christ was referring to himself, not to Peter, as the rock, the foundation for his Church. Fundamentalists base this claim on 1 Corinthians 10:4:

> . . . and all drank the same supernatural drink. For they drank from the supernatural Rock which followed them, and the Rock was Christ.

If Jesus was referring to himself when he says, "upon this rock I build my church," then he was not speaking very clearly. Here's a further explanation:

> Matthew must have realized that his readers would conclude the obvious from "Rock . . . rock". If he meant Christ to be understood as the rock, why did he not say so? Why did he construct his sentences so awkwardly that contortions would be required to elicit the fundamentalist interpretation? Why did he take a chance and leave it up to Paul to write a clarifying text . . . ?
>
> The reason, of course, is that Matthew knew full well that what the sentence seemed to say was just what it really was saying. It was Simon—weak, Christ-denying Simon—who was chosen to be the first link in the chain of the papacy. The scandal, to fundamentalists, is that Christ would choose as his vicar the weakest of the apostles, not the strongest. But God seems to enjoy working through the lowly in order to confound the mighty, and his choice of Peter was quite in keeping with other selections he had made, such as deciding to be born in a stable rather than a palace. In a way, it was Peter's weakness that would manifest the strength of the papacy. After all, noted G. K. Chesterton when writing of the succession of popes, a chain is only as strong as its weakest link.[2]

Aside from the question of what Jesus meant when he called Peter *rock* we have other examples in Scripture to show us that Peter was the intended head of his Church.

[2] Karl Keating, *Catholicism and Fundamentalism* (San Francisco: Ignatius Press, 1988), p. 211.

On the night before he died, at the Last Supper, Jesus prayed that Peter would have faith that would not fail and be a guide for the others:

> "Simon, Simon, behold, Satan demanded to have you, that he might sift you [the Greek is plural for "you" here, referring to all the apostles] like wheat, but I have prayed for you [the Greek is singular here, referring to Peter specifically] that your faith may not fail; and when you have turned again, strengthen your brethren."

Jesus singles Peter out from the group here.

Peter replied, "Lord, I am ready to go with you to prison and to death." But Jesus, fully aware of the weakness in the one he had chosen to strengthen the others, predicted: "I tell you, Peter, the cock will not crow this day, until you three times deny that you know me" (Lk 22:31–34).

After he rose from the dead, Jesus asked Peter three times, in reparation for his three denials, "Simon, son of John, do you love me?" Peter responded, "Yes, Lord, you know that I love you." Three times Peter affirmed his love for Christ. After Peter's affirmations, Jesus, who is himself the "Good Shepherd," said to Peter, "Feed my lambs. . . . Tend my sheep. . . . Feed my sheep" (Jn 21:15–17).

Jesus made Peter the leader, putting him in charge of the Church. When the apostles gathered with others of the new Christian community to name a replacement for Judas, it was Peter who headed up the meeting. "In those days Peter stood up among the brethren" (Acts 1:15). He explained that Scripture was fulfilled in Judas, and quoted a psalm of David to indicate that Judas was to be replaced: "His office let another take." Likewise, on Pentecost, it was Peter who first began preaching to the crowds:

> But Peter, standing with the eleven, lifted up his voice and addressed them, "Men of Judea and all who dwell in Jerusalem, let this be known to you, and give ear to my words" (Acts 2:14).

"Then after three years I went up to Jerusalem to visit Cephas, and remained with him fifteen days" (Gal 1:18). These are Paul's words. Before beginning his mission he went to Peter, the head of the Church.

In Acts 3, Peter and John go to the temple together. A man crippled from birth asks them for an alms. Again it is Peter who takes the lead, does the talking and performs the miracle.

It is Peter who is given the revelation that Gentiles as well as Jews are to be baptized into the Church. "Then Peter declared, 'Can anyone forbid the water for baptizing these people who have received the Holy Spirit just as we have?' And he commanded them to be baptized in the name of Jesus Christ" (Acts 10:46–48). Here we have Peter making a monumental decision and giving a command. Throughout the New Testament we have numerous examples of Peter speaking for the Apostles. (See Mt 18:21, Mk 8:29, Lk 12:41, Jn 6:69.)

Wherever the apostles are listed in Scripture, Peter is always listed first (see Mt 10:2, Mk 3:16, Lk 6:14, and Acts 1:13). In the New Testament, Peter's name is mentioned 179 times. The next most frequently mentioned apostle is John, mentioned thirty times. All the apostles combined, minus Peter, are mentioned a total of 149 times.

Peter was the first chosen leader, but Jesus also chose his successors and conferred on them all the appropriate powers. Jesus did not establish a church merely for his contemporaries. We need to keep the Church just as Jesus gave it to us. He sent the apostles to teach all nations and said he would be with them until the end of time, so the hierarchy he established, logically, was to last as long as his Church—until the end of time. Jesus gave Peter the keys of the kingdom of heaven; he gave him authority. If this is how he set up his Church, isn't this the way he wants it to be? For those against having a pope, does Scripture designate some alternative organization of the Church once Peter died? No, it does not.

Although there are those who criticize the papacy, the position of pope cannot be changed. It is a matter of dogma that the pope is the successor of Peter and holds primacy in the Church. The will of Christ regarding his Church cannot be changed and Church leaders will never attempt to do so.

The First Vatican Council, 1869–1870, defined the dogma of papal infallibility. It reaffirmed that, when carrying out his duty as pastor and teacher of all Christians, the pope, by virtue of his authority, is infallible when he defines a doctrine of faith or morals to be held by all the faithful. A century later, the Second Vatican Council reaffirmed these teachings but added emphasis on the infallibility of the "ordinary magisterium," the bishops of the world in union with the pope, teaching in union with one another.

History tells us that Peter was martyred in Rome after heading the Church there. Modern excavations found bones, which evidence indicates are those of Peter, buried under St. Peter's Basilica at the Vatican. Many historical writings confirm that Peter was the first pope. Some anti-Catholics say Peter's power was never passed on because they claim there is no record of any pope from St. Peter's death until the fourth century. But this is untrue. During the second century, St. Irenaeus, Bishop of Lyons, gave the list of the popes from St. Peter until his day. The Roman Catholic Church has a detailed documented list of the succession of popes from Peter to the present.

> Writing to contentious Christians in the Greek city of Corinth midway through the last decade of the first century, Pope St. Clement I, Peter's third successor, delivered a stiff rebuke. The Bishop of Rome decried "impious and detestable sedition" on the part of some and urged them to obey the leaders of the local church.
>
> "But if some will not submit to them," Pope Clement added, "let them learn what he [Christ] has spoken through us, that they will involve themselves in great sin and danger."
>
> For a long time, the First Epistle of Clement to the Corinthians has been considered the earliest existing evidence after apostolic times of the exercise of papal primacy, albeit in a primitive form.[3]

Peter lived in Rome and presided over the Church from Rome. By calling it the Roman Catholic Church, we are recognizing the pope as the acting head of the universal Church on earth. Catholic means universal. To digress a moment, this is where we part

[3] Russell Shaw, "Why the Pope Rules," *Our Sunday Visitor*, February 22, 1998.

ways with Orthodox churches. The Orthodox churches have been in schism with the Roman Catholic Church since 1054. Though they accept all the doctrines of the Roman Catholic Church, they do not accept the authority of the pope. Other faiths are considered in heresy because they reject doctrines of the Church.

The Orthodox churches are separated from total unity with the pope, but they still have a valid priesthood. This means that their Eucharist celebration does change bread and wine into the Body and Blood of Christ. The reason is that when the churches divided, they took validly ordained bishops with them. Validly ordained bishops trace their powers back to the original apostles and to Jesus Christ. This is referred to as Apostolic Succession or the Apostolic Chain. Bishops have the power to ordain new priests and other bishops and therefore continue the apostolic succession. Only a validly ordained bishop can ordain priests and hand down the special powers God grants to his priests. The passing on of this power is mentioned in Scripture: "Hence I remind you to rekindle the gift of God that is within you through the laying on of my hands" (2 Tim 1:6).

The pope speaks as the head and in unity with the college of bishops. The Church, through the pope, speaks with authority not from itself, but from God. God wants us to live in truth. We cannot live in truth without an infallible guide. The Roman Catholic Church, under the infallible leadership of the pope, is that guide.

Catholics and non-Catholics alike are often confused by what it means to teach infallibly. Infallibility means to be preserved immune from error. It doesn't mean the pope knows everything and it also does not mean that a pope is incapable of sinning. It is the gift Christ gave his Church, the supernatural assistance of the Holy Spirit, to protect the Church from error. Teaching authority is given to the apostles by Jesus. In order to teach, the Church must do so free from error, or its teachings would oppose those of Jesus and the gates of hell would have prevailed.

Specific conditions must be met for the pope formally to teach infallibly, or ex cathedra. (1) He must be teaching on matters of faith or morals. (2) He must say that he is speaking as the Roman Pontiff, the head of the Church, and using his authority as such.

(3) He must make it clear that he is teaching infallibly on a matter which is to be held by all the faithful. (4) The teaching must be formulated publicly and universally and made known as an infallible teaching.

It was during the great councils of the Church that some of the teachings that had been part of Church history from the beginning were presented infallibly in a more formal way. An example of this is the Catholic belief in transubstantiation. This belief teaches that the bread and wine are completely changed into the substance of Christ's Body and Blood by the words of a validly ordained priest during the consecration at Mass, so only the appearance of bread and wine remain. This process, often referred to as "transubstantiation," was already believed in apostolic times. For over ten centuries, nobody questioned the Real Presence of Christ in the Eucharist. Christians accepted Biblical and Church teachings in this matter, but it was formally restated as a Church doctrine in 1215 at the Fourth Lateran Council as a response to false teachings denying the True Presence, which had begun to spread. At this time the term "transubstantiation" was used to state the doctrine clearly.

Because these pronouncements are given at a particular point in history, anti-Catholics sometimes accuse the Church of inventing infallible teachings and give dates for these new teachings. For example, fundamentalists claim Catholics made up the doctrine of the Immaculate Conception, that Mary, as the future vessel for Jesus, was pure from the start—conceived without original sin on her soul. This doctrine was officially defined in 1854. When detractors say it was invented then, they ignore the history of dogmas and the reasons the Church issues definitive teachings from time to time. In reality, these doctrines were always believed but were only officially declared at a particular time, sometimes in response to the promotion of false teachings or because the magisterium (pope and bishops) believe the faithful can be helped by emphasis on an already existing belief. The infallible teaching on the Immaculate Conception was given by Pope Pius IX, who was devoted to the Blessed Mother and hoped the formal definition would inspire others to draw closer to her and thereby to her son, Jesus.

The pope ordinarily does not exercise the gift of infallibility alone. Jesus gave teaching authority also to the apostles with primacy given to Peter. The college of bishops, acting with the pope as its head, can proclaim a teaching authoritatively. This happens when the pope calls the bishops of the world together and their final conclusions become the official teachings of the Roman Catholic Church.

Bishops and priests, other religious, and lay persons can all use their talents to teach and evangelize. But in order for the faith to be kept in truth, all teachings must be in agreement with the declared teachings of the Church under the pope and her bishops. Consider that when Jesus gave Peter and the apostles authority, he told them that whatever they held bound on earth would be bound in heaven and whatever they loosed on earth, would be loosed in heaven. This is another reason why the Church must be kept free from error. Infallibility is not an option for his Church but a necessity. The Church God established will follow his lead, not the other way around.

Anyone who says he is a Catholic and then teaches something that is not in agreement with the Church's infallibly declared positions is not in union with the Church and may even be ipso facto excommunicated. In today's Church, it is not hard to find Catholics espousing teachings opposed to official Catholic doctrine. If you want truth, however, seek the truth Jesus guaranteed us through the Church leadership he designated.

The scandalous behavior of some popes, especially in the Middle Ages, is occasionally brought up as evidence that the office of the pope could not be infallible and has no rightful leadership in the Church. Yes, it's true that there have been some bad leaders in Church history, but that should not surprise or scandalize us. We are all sinners, and Jesus showed us from the start that sinfulness in the whole world and in the Church is a part of life. He allowed a sinner—Judas—to be a part of his inner circle. We know that a pope can teach truth, such as that stealing is a sin, and then steal himself, but that does not make his teaching false. Although there have been popes in history whose personal lives were immoral, for almost two thousand years of Church history, no pope has ever taught a doctrine of faith or morals that contradicted previous Church teaching. Out of the 265 popes our Church has had, only a small number have behaved improperly. Yet, even these men never taught heresy while they were popes. Jesus promised to keep his Church in truth; this is the gift of infallibility. It is this gift of the Holy Spirit that guarantees us, that regardless of their righteousness or lack thereof, no pope can propose a teaching contrary to revealed truth or Church doctrine.

In spite of some corruption, the Church has always had clearly appointed leaders. Organizations flounder without leadership, and it is unbiblical to think that the church should be run as a democracy. Christ never called for a *majority rules* consensus, or asked for opposing viewpoints. It was just the opposite. He was a teacher, and the people admired and followed him because he taught with authority (see Mk 1:22).

The scribes and the Pharisees (the leaders of the Jewish people at the time) often openly disagreed with our Lord and opposed his teaching, partly because he was correcting their misinterpretation of the Old Law. Some times they stirred up the people to disagree with him. And even occasionally some of his followers found aspects of his teaching difficult to understand and embrace, and they ceased following him. (See Jn 6:41, 53, 61, 67.)

Public opinion or changing times had absolutely nothing to do with the truth he taught. Jesus never took a vote.. So those who say the pope is an unmarried man, unable to understand the stresses of family life, out of step with today's world, and unwilling to bend to the will and opinions of the people, would not be saying anything different than was said of Jesus. Those criticisms are actually additional verification that, indeed, the pope is God's chosen leader for his Church, acting in place of Jesus.

8

THE EUCHARIST

When I walk into a Catholic Church and kneel before the tabernacle containing the Eucharist, I am kneeling in the true presence of God in a way not possible anywhere else. It is the Eucharist that urges me to instill Catholicism in my children. They could grow up to be good members of society and believe in Jesus Christ, but without the Eucharist, they would be missing out on the greatest gift Jesus gave to us—himself, his own flesh and blood, which he sacrificed for our sake and gave to us at the Last Supper.

We need to educate our children about the Eucharist to protect them against attacks on the Real Presence. Although recent polls indicate a majority of Catholics still believe that Christ is truly present in the species of bread and wine upon consecration, there are some Catholics who do not. But this is a key element of our faith. How we respond to receiving the actual Body and Blood of our Lord and Savior, God himself, should be radically different from what our response would be to receiving a symbolic bread wafer.

Before I completely accepted all of the teachings of the Catholic Church, there were times when our family attended Sunday services of other denominations. Usually we were camping and there was a nondenominational service at the campground or nearby that was more convenient than searching out a Catholic Mass. Typically, the singing was beautiful and the preachers were enthusiastic.

As I grew in understanding of my faith, these services became more and more hollow to me, until one Sunday, I walked away from one leaving my husband, Mark, behind. "I'm going to evening Mass when we return home," I said to him. At the time Mark thought I was being narrow-minded and judgmental when I expressed my opinion that the service was shallow and off track. Eventually, however, we grew together in our faith and became of one mind.

Nowadays, neither Mark nor I would ever substitute another denomination's service for the Mass because the Eucharist commits us to the Catholic Church. Aside from differences in form and style, the crux of what is lacking for us is the Eucharist. We have come to realize what an awesome gift it is and would never choose to go without it. Because we take to heart our Lord's words, we believe that he is truly present and comes to us personally in the Eucharist. We fully believe Jesus meant what He said: "Truly, truly, I say to you, unless you eat the flesh of the Son of Man and drink his blood, you have no life in you" (Jn 6:53) and also, "My flesh is food indeed, and my blood is drink indeed" (Jn 6:55).

> Now as they were eating, Jesus took bread, and blessed, and broke it, and gave it to the disciples and said, "Take, eat; this is my body." And he took a cup, and when he had given thanks he gave it to them, saying, "Drink of it, all of you; for this is my blood of the covenant, which is poured out for many for the forgiveness of sins" (Mt 26:26–28).

> And as they were eating, he took bread, and blessed, and broke it, and gave it to them, and said, "Take; this is my body." And he took a cup, and when he had given thanks he gave it to them, and they all drank of it. And he said to them, "This is my blood of the covenant, which is poured out for many" (Mk 14:22–24).

> And he took a cup, and when he had given thanks he said, "Take this and divide it among yourselves; for I tell you that from now on I shall not drink of the fruit of the vine until the kingdom of God comes." And he took bread, and when he had given thanks he broke it and gave it to them, saying, "This is my body which is given for you. Do this in remembrance of me" (Lk 22:17–19).

> For I received from the Lord what I also delivered to you, that the Lord Jesus on the night when he was betrayed took bread, and when he had given thanks, he broke it and said, "This is my body which is for you. Do this in

> remembrance of me." In the same way also the cup, after supper, saying, "This cup is the new covenant in my blood. Do this, as often as you drink it, in remembrance of me" (1 Cor 11:23–24).

Virtually all the Protestant denominations believe Christ is present only symbolically. This is the reason that when their church offers communion, visitors from other denominations are welcome to partake. The Catholic Church does not allow non-Catholics to receive Holy Communion at a Catholic Mass and is often criticized for being snobbish and not fully embracing people from outside the faith. But if others understood the truth of this most holy Sacrament, they would understand that it is not ours to give. We cannot offer it to those who do not believe that Jesus is fully present in the Eucharist, without offending God.

St. Paul warned the Corinthians against receiving the Eucharist unworthily:

> Whoever, therefore, eats the bread or drinks the cup of the Lord in an unworthy manner will be guilty of profaning the body and blood of the Lord. Let a man examine himself, and so eat of the bread and drink of the cup. For any one who eats and drinks without discerning the body eats and drinks judgment upon himself (1 Cor 11:27–29).

Would eating a piece of bread bear such serious consequences? Just prior to his warning, St. Paul explains why we must be worthy of receiving the Eucharist. "The cup of blessing which we bless, is it not a participation in the blood of Christ? The bread which we break, is it not a participation in the body of Christ?" (1 Cor 10:16).

In the above passages of the Bible, we are told that Christ is truly present in the bread and wine. This has been taught and written about since the Last Supper. Why then do some Christians scoff at Catholics and accuse us of worshiping bread wafers? It's the same reason that some of Christ's own followers left him when he told them, "I am the living bread which came down from heaven; if any one eats of this bread, he will live for ever; and the bread which I shall give for the life of the world is my flesh" (Jn 6:51).

It is a difficult teaching to accept and embrace. It takes a lot of faith, confidence in God and humility. For some, it's just too hard to accept. So, like those who physically walked away during Christ's time on earth, people intellectually walk away from it today invoking the word symbolic. "Christ is only symbolically present," we are told. "Don't you know when and when not to interpret the Bible literally?" We can use the Bible in this instance to show Christ was not speaking symbolically.

> In the Aramaic language that our Lord spoke, to symbolically "eat the flesh" or "drink the blood" of someone meant to persecute and assault him. See Ps 27:2; Is 9:18–20; Is 49:26; Mic 3:3; 2 Sam 23:15–17; and Rev 17:6, 16. Thus, if Jesus were only speaking symbolically about eating his flesh and drinking his blood, as Protestants say, then what he really meant was "whoever persecutes and assaults me will have eternal life." This, of course, makes nonsense of the passage![1]

Jesus does, however, use food symbolically at times:

> Jesus said to them, "My food is to do the will of him who sent me, and to accomplish his work" (Jn 4:34).

> "How is it that you fail to perceive that I did not speak about bread? Beware of the leaven of the Pharisees and Sadducees." Then they understood that he did not tell them to beware of the leaven of bread, but of the teaching of the Pharisees and Sadducees (Mt 16:11–12).

In both the above cases, Jesus was at first mistakenly taken as speaking about real food, when in fact, he was using food symbolically. But it is important to take note that Jesus clears up the misunderstanding and makes sure his meaning is clear.

Now compare that with the repeated teachings of Christ in John 6, where Jesus reiterates that the food he speaks of is his own flesh and blood:

---

[1] Fr. Frank Chacon and Jim Burnham, *Beginning Apologetics 1* (Farmington, N.M.: San Juan Catholic Seminars, 1998), p. 8.

> "I am the living bread which came down from heaven; if any one eats of this bread, he will live for ever; and the bread which I will give for the life of the world is my flesh."
>
> The Jews quarreled among themselves saying, "How can this man give us his flesh to eat?" So Jesus said to them, "Truly, truly, I say to you, unless you eat the flesh of the Son of man and drink his blood, you have no life in you; he who eats my flesh and drinks my blood has eternal life, and I will raise him at the last day. For my flesh is food indeed, and my blood is drink indeed. He who eats my flesh and drinks my blood abides in me and I in him. As the living Father sent me, and I live because of the Father, so he who eats me will live because of me" (Jn 6:51–57).

Jesus lays it on the line quite clearly. When even some of his own disciples said this teaching is hard to accept, Jesus asked, "Do you take offense at this?" (Jn 6:61). It shocked many to the extent that they ceased to follow Jesus and returned to their former ways and lives. Since Jesus cleared up misunderstandings previously, it would not make sense for him intentionally to leave his followers confused and watch them depart over a mistaken definition. But rather, he made it clear that he meant what he said. He let those who could not accept his teaching leave.

> Many Protestants claim that, in John 6:60–70, Jesus explains that he was only speaking symbolically in the previous verses. They focus on verse 63, "It is the spirit that gives life, the flesh is of no avail; the words I have spoken to you are spirit and life." Be prepared to deal with this objection as follows:
>
> (*a*) Jesus' Eucharistic talk ends with verse 58 (see verse 59). The dialogue of verses 60–70 occurs later and deals with faith, not the Eucharist.
>
> (*b*) The word "spirit" is nowhere used in the Bible to mean "symbolic." The spiritual is just as real as the material.
>
> (*c*) In verse 63, Jesus is contrasting the natural or carnal man ("the flesh") with the spiritual or faith-filled man. Read 1 Corinthians 2:14—3:4 for a good explanation of

what Jesus means by "the flesh." Note that Jesus says "my flesh" when discussing the Eucharist. He says "the flesh" when referring to the carnal man who will not believe anything beyond his senses and reason. No Christian believes that Jesus' flesh is "of no avail," for his flesh was the means of our redemption.

(*d*) Note that the unbelieving disciples leave Jesus after verse 63—they would not have left at this point if Jesus had assured them that he was only speaking symbolically. This is the only time recorded in the New Testament that any of Jesus' disciples left him because they found a doctrine of his too hard to accept. Of the twelve Apostles, apparently only Judas rejected the Eucharist (Jn 6: 70–71).[2]

Another line of argument against Jesus speaking literally is to say that when Jesus said, "this is my body" or "blood," the Bible translates it in Greek as *touto esti.* The claim is that *touto esti* can only mean "this represents or stands for." That is not true.

> *Esti* is nothing else than the verb "is". Its usual meaning is the literal, although it can be used figuratively, just as in English. If this crucial term is supposed to be read as "represents", why was it not clearly put so in the Greek?[3]

The charge of symbolism is further pushed by the fact that Christ did sometimes speak figuratively and used symbols to represent himself. For instance, "I am the door" (Jn 10: 9), or "I am the true vine" (Jn 15: 1). The difference between these symbols and Jesus' teaching on the Eucharist was explained by Leslie Rumble and Charles M. Carty, who once moderated a Catholic radio program called Radio Replies:

> There is no logical parallel between the words "This is My body" and "I am the vine" or "I am the door." For the images of the vine and door can have, of their very nature, a symbolic sense. Christ is like a vine because all the sap of

[2] Ibid., pp. 7–8.

[3] Keating, *Catholicism and Fundamentalism* (San Francisco: Ignatius Press, 1988), p. 235.

> my spiritual life comes from Him. He is like a door since I go to heaven through Him. But a piece of bread is in no way like his flesh. Of its very nature it cannot symbolize the actual body of Christ And he excludes that Himself by saying, "The bread that I will give is My flesh for the life of the world, and My flesh is meat indeed." That it is to be actually eaten, not merely commemorated in some symbolical way.[4]

Yet another claim against the bread and wine becoming the Body and Blood of Christ is that Catholics attempt to re-sacrifice Christ again at every Mass. After all, it is referred to as the Holy Sacrifice of the Mass. Scripture says: "But when Christ had offered for all time a single sacrifice for sins, he sat down at the right hand of God, then to wait until his enemies should be made a stool for his feet. For by a single offering he has perfected for all time those who are sanctified" (Heb 10: 12–14).

What this attack fails to understand is that Catholics fully agree that there was only one sacrifice, the sacrifice to end all sacrifices—the death of Jesus Christ on the cross. We do not sacrifice Jesus over again at Mass. Rather, the sacrifice is re-presented.[5] We are made present at the foot of the cross on Calvary. Through the Mass, we pray to God the Father through Jesus Christ, who continually makes present to us his sacrifice, and then invites us to receive him—the bread of life.

> The Passover sacrifice was not considered complete until the people had eaten the Passover lamb, whose blood, sprinkled on the doorposts and lintels of their homes, protected them from the Angel of Death. In the same way Jesus Christ our Lord, the true Lamb of God (cf. Jn 1:29, 36), invites us to partake of the sacrificial Eucharistic meal, his own Body and Blood. He promised this gift to his disciples (cf. Jn 6: 22–71), and he fulfilled his promise in the institution of the Eucharist at the Last Supper when he gave them his Body and Blood to eat and drink as the true Passover Lamb that would be sacrificed.[6]

---

[4] Fathers Rumble and Carty, *Radio Replies* (Rockford, Ill.: Tan Books, 1979).

[5] *Catechism of the Catholic Church*, no. 1366.

[6] Julie Swenson, in Patrick Madrid, *Surprised by Truth*, p. 152.

Scripture predicted just such a sacrifice as we celebrate at our Catholic Mass:

> The Old Testament predicted that Christ would offer a true sacrifice to God in bread and wine—that he would use those elements. Melchisedech, the king of Salem and a priest, offered sacrifice under the form of bread and wine (Gen 14:18). Psalm 110 predicted Christ would be a priest, "according to the order of Melchisedech", that is, offering a sacrifice in bread and wine. We must, then, look for some sacrifice other than Calvary, since it was not under the form of bread and wine. The Mass fits the bill.[7]

One final accusation against the Eucharist, which was mentioned in chapter 7 but is relevant to this teaching, is the charge that Catholics made up the whole thing in 1215 A.D. when Pope Innocent made use of the term "transubstantiation"—the technical word used to describe the event of the bread and wine being turned into the Body and Blood of Christ.

The accusation claims "transubstantiation" was unheard of prior to that date. In part, they are correct. Just as the term "Trinity" appears nowhere in the Bible, the term "transubstantiation" was indeed "made up." It was coined to describe the occurrence that all Catholics at that time believed to take place when an ordained priest, acting in the role of Christ, consecrated the elements of bread and wine using the words of Jesus Christ to make him fully present to us. The term "transubstantiation" was used to explain the Real Presence of Jesus in bread and wine. It was formally chosen at the Fourth Lateran Council in the year 1215. It was indeed a new term, not used previously, but it was not a new doctrine.

The *Catechism of the Catholic Church* explains:

> The Council of Trent summarizes the Catholic faith by declaring: "Because Christ our Redeemer said that it was truly his body that he was offering under the species of bread, it has always been the conviction of the Church of God, and this holy Council now declares again, that by

[7] Keating, *Catholicism and Fundamentalism*, p. 253.

> the consecration of the bread and wine there takes place a change of the whole substance of the bread into the substance of the body of Christ our Lord and of the whole substance of the wine into the substance of his blood. This change the holy Catholic Church has fittingly and properly called transubstantiation.[8]

To confirm that the doctrine existed since the earliest days of the Church, one has merely to check history and find out what the early Church leaders taught. Two important early Christians were St. Ignatius of Antioch and St. Irenaeus. St. Ignatius's life was partly contemporaneous with that of the apostle St. John, and he is said to have been a disciple of John. Addressing the Christians in Smyrnea, he speaks of some heretics, who "do not admit that the Eucharist is the Flesh of our Savior Jesus Christ, the flesh which suffered for our sins and which the Father, in his graciousness, raised from the dead."[9] In another letter he wrote, "Be zealous, then, in the observance of one Eucharist. For there is one flesh of our Lord Jesus Christ and one chalice that brings union in his blood."[10] Toward the end of the second century, St. Irenaeus, the bishop of Lyons, who is considered the Father of Theology, spoke of the Eucharist in the following terms: "The bread, which is produced from the earth, when it receives the invocation of God, is no longer common bread, but the Eucharist . . .", and "He [Jesus] has declared the cup, a part of creation, to be his own Blood, from which he causes our blood to flow; and the bread, a part of creation, he has established as his own Body, from which he gives increase to our bodies."[11]

Karl Keating, in his book *Catholicism and Fundamentalism*, likewise provides numerous quotes from the early Church Fathers expressing strong faith in the Real Presence of Christ in the Eucharist. Catholic bookstores, catalogs, and university libraries abound with books containing writings of the early Church Fathers which support this teaching. If anyone needs

---

[8] *Catechism of the Catholic Church*, no. 1376; Council of Trent (1551): DS 1642; cf. Mt 26:26ff.; Mk 14:22ff.; Lk 22:19ff.; 1 Cor 11:24ff.

[9] St. Ignatius of Antioch, *Letter to the Smyrneans*, 6, 2.

[10] St. Ignatius of Antioch, *Letter to the Romans*, 7:3.

[11] St. Irenaeus, *Adversus Haereses*, 5, 2, 2.

further proof that Jesus Christ is truly present in the Eucharist, they owe it to themselves to do the research.

Every time we receive the Eucharist we participate in the most important event in the history of the world. The sacrifice of love that gives us our salvation is being re-presented every day, around the world at Mass. When we meditate on the fact that God himself is coming to us personally in the Eucharist, it should leave us awestruck and overwhelmingly appreciative. We should want our children to receive this gift frequently. That is why it is so very important that no one be able to talk them out of it. We can't let them miss out on receiving Jesus because someone convinced them he is not really there.

During the consecration, when the priest lifts up the bread and wine and it becomes the Body and Blood, I sometimes need to remind my little ones to be quiet or kneel up straight because "Jesus is coming now." I know my children don't fully comprehend the enormity of it all, but then, neither do I. I try to put myself in the right frame of mind and appreciate all I'm being given, but I know I can't even begin to fathom what it truly means to be receiving God. But I do know that he is there, not by sight but by faith. We need to pass the same faith onto our children that kept the apostles at Jesus' side when he asked them, "Will you also go away?" (Jn 6:67).

Peter answered, "Lord, to whom shall we go? You have the words of eternal life" (Jn 6:68). Peter didn't say, "Hey, it all makes sense to me, Lord." He didn't fully understand what it all meant, but he had faith in Jesus Christ and knew that, even if he couldn't always make sense out of his teachings, Jesus had the full truth and the words of eternal life. Likewise, when we look at the elements of bread and wine and our eyes see only bread and wine, we must rely on our faith to accept that Jesus is truly present, Body and Blood to us, when we receive him in the Eucharist.

When preparing a child for his first Holy Communion, I think one of the more important things we can do is read to him the Gospel of John, chapter 6, and then discuss what was happening. Then read the four passages that record the Last Supper.

Even a second grader can understand what it means to use something as a symbol—for example, the flag symbolizes our country, or a dollar sign symbolizes money. You can explain that some people thought Jesus didn't mean what he said, that it was just a symbol. Tell them that Jesus did sometimes use symbols to help people understand what he was trying to tell them, but each time he either explained what he meant by the symbol, or else the symbol was something with which everyone was familiar. Tell them that bread was never a symbol for a person's flesh, and furthermore, Jesus repeated the message four times that his flesh was real food.

Let your children know that this is a very hard teaching to understand and that even adults don't know exactly how Jesus makes it possible for us to truly receive him under the form of bread and wine. Neither do we understand how God created the universe and could have existed forever without a beginning. There is a lot we don't understand and that is why we must always thank God for his gift of faith to us and also to ask him to increase our faith.

Even a young child can learn what the word "transubstantiation" means and that the Catholic Church came up with that word to explain the event of bread and wine becoming the Body and Blood of Jesus. Tell them that some people mistakenly think the Catholic Church made up this teaching, but that is wrong. They made up the word then, not the teaching. The teaching is that when the bread and wine are consecrated by a bishop or priest, Jesus becomes truly present. We still see the bread and wine, but through faith we believe they have been transformed into his Body and Blood.

Although sometimes Communion is distributed under both species, even if you only receive the Host, Jesus is still fully present. He is completely present in the smallest drop of consecrated wine or in the smallest fragment of the consecrated bread. Keep in mind that Jesus talked about receiving under both species but also of receiving him in the bread alone: "He who eats this bread will live for ever" (Jn 6:58).

The Church teaches that in order to receive the Eucharist worthily, we must be old enough to appreciate that we are receiving Jesus, be baptized, have no mortal sin on our soul and be sorry for our venial sins, have fasted for one hour before Holy Communion (except medicine or water) and we should desire to receive the Eucharist and not be going just out of habit or to join the crowd.

If your children believe God is present in the Eucharist, they won't need to go anywhere else to find Him. They won't need fancy church performances or lively scenes from the pulpit. Regardless of what might be less than perfect at Mass; be it bad singing, a sleepwalking congregation, or a lackluster sermon, there will always be something worthwhile there—the gift of Jesus Christ made present to us.

9

CONFESSION

Confession (also known as Penance and Reconciliation) is probably for many a much overlooked and infrequently used gift. Through this sacrament we live our faith, learn humility to face another with our failings, make an examination of conscience, confess our sins, and receive absolution, spiritual guidance, and the grace to help us avoid future sin. This is a rich experience that deepens our spirituality and draws us closer to God. It is an opportunity to grow; it is not a punishment.

> It is called the sacrament of conversion because it makes sacramentally present Jesus' call to conversion, the first step in returning to the Father (cf. Mk 1: 15; Lk 15: 18) from whom one has strayed by sin . . . (CCC, no. 1423).[1]

> Sin is before all else an offense against God, a rupture of communion with him. At the same time it damages communion with the Church. For this reason, conversion entails both God's forgiveness and reconciliation with the Church, which are expressed and accomplished liturgically by the sacrament of Penance and Reconciliation (cf. *Lumen Gentium* 11) (CCC, no. 1440).

Thus far, I've attended parents' meetings for five of my children preparing to receive the sacrament of Reconciliation. I've noticed several questions that commonly come up among parents. One is that young children are not capable of committing a mortal sin, so why should they go to confession?

The reason young children are encouraged to receive this sacrament was explained in a 1986 communication to the U.S. bishops from the Vatican Congregation for Divine Worship and the Discipline of the Sacraments.

---

[1] CCC is the *Catechism of the Catholic Church.*

> The basis for this observance, for children, is not so much the state of sin in which they may be . . . (but) to educate them, from a tender age, to the true Christian spirit of penance and conversion, to growth in self-knowledge and self-control, to a just sense of sin, even of venial sin, to the necessity of asking for pardon of God and above all to a loving and confident abandonment to the mercy of the Lord.[2]

Another issue which may cause some resistance among parents is the fact that they themselves may not have gone to Confession in a long time and are uncomfortable with the Sacrament.

I have heard a number of friends speak of how nervous they were about going to Confession after years of absence. I too have such a story. I am going to share mine with you, so if you are hesitant to return to the sacrament, it might help you to think, "Well, I cannot do any worse than she did."

I went fifteen or more years without confession because I regarded it as unnecessary. One Sunday, a church we attended in Kalispell, Montana, announced that there would be a group confession later that week. I have since learned that this sacrament can be administered to a group only under dire emergencies (such as war), usually with permission from the bishop. Although I did not recognize it at the time, this particular church did a lot of things that were not in accordance with Catholic teaching.

At any rate, it struck me as a painless way to return to the sacrament of Confession. (Each person waits in a long line and then tells one sin to save time and then absolution is given to the whole crowd.) I attended the service and then felt relieved that I had the whole unpleasant business so easily out of the way.

Around this time, however, I began studying Catholicism. I learned that Jesus gave the apostles the power to forgive sins when he appeared to them on Easter Sunday, the day he rose from the dead. He gave them the power to cleanse our souls, which only God can do, and fill us with graces that bring us closer to him and help us not to sin again. I began to desire the

---

[2] Msgr. M. Francis Mannion, "Pastoral Answers," *Our Sunday Visitor*, June 15, 1997.

sacrament of Confession to be in fuller union with God. Since it had been at least fifteen years since I had seen the inside of a confessional, I also had my share of reluctance.

Shortly afterward we moved to Bismarck, North Dakota. One Saturday afternoon, I finally decided to go to Confession. I walked into the church and nervously waited until it was my turn to enter the confessional. My heart pounded, and to make matters worse, the small enclosure was pitch black; I mean pitch. I wondered why they kept it so dark. Then, I heard a door on the other side open and close. Horrified, I realized the priest (who had to get ready for 5 o'clock Mass) had just left the confessional, probably not realizing I was in there.

So there I sat, alone, in a completely dark confessional. "If I walk out now," I surmised, "he'll see me coming out of the empty confessional and I'll be so embarrassed." I purposely had chosen the separate room so I would not have to face the priest directly. "But if I stay a few minutes, people in church will wonder what I was doing so long in an empty confessional," I thought.

I chose to wait a few minutes until the priest was safely gone. As I emerged, my first instinct was to run to the car and forget the whole thing. Instead, I decided I had dragged myself this far so I should go through with it. I waited in line for the next priest, got through it just fine, felt relieved and cleansed and have lived to tell about it. I now go regularly. Now that it has become a habit, I actually look forward to going.

The Catholic Church recommends daily examination of conscience and saying sorry to God for our sins before retiring at the end of the day. The sacrament of Confession is required of anyone guilty of serious sin—mortal sin–before receiving Holy Communion. Mortal sin separates us from God by destroying sanctifying grace in our souls. It is spiritual death; loss of the soul's sanctifying grace. Confession brings our soul back to life in Christ.

The Church teaches that for a sin to be mortal, it must be a grave matter which is committed with full awareness and deliberate intention.

Not all denominations recognize there are two kinds of sin—mortal and venial. But the Catholic teaching is supported in Scripture:

> Now the works of the flesh are plain: immorality, impurity, licentiousness, idolatry, sorcery, enmity, strife, jealousy, anger, selfishness, dissensions, party spirit, envy, drunkenness, carousing, and the like. I warn you, as I warned you before, that those who do such things shall not inherit the kingdom of God (Gal 5: 19–21).

> If any one sees his brother committing what is not a mortal sin, he will ask, and God will give him life for those whose sin is not mortal. There is sin which is not mortal; I do not say that one is to pray for that. All wrongdoing is sin, but there is sin that is not mortal (1 Jn 5: 16–17).

The confession of venial sins is not necessary but is strongly recommended by the Church as a way to make reparation and strengthen ourselves spiritually. Venial sin weakens charity within us and interferes with the soul's progress. It erodes our friendship with Christ but does not destroy it. The further our relationship with him is eroded, however, the greater the likelihood that we will fall into mortal sin.

As I prepared my children for their first Confession, I was pleased to see they looked forward to it. When Luke told me he had a light, happy feeling after Confession and Aaron agreed he did too, I was again pleased. By the time I was preparing son number 3, Tyler, it began to dawn on me that the happy, light feeling could fade away one day just like so much of the magic of childhood fades into adolescence.

If that light, happy feeling was not there one day, would my children still love the sacrament by understanding why and how God gave it to us? They needed to understand the biblical reasons Catholics believe in the truth and power of this sacrament. If one day a college roommate says, "There is one mediator between God and men, the man Christ Jesus (1 Tim 2: 5), so you are way off base going to a priest," would my kids have an explanation for why they went to a priest for forgiveness? I realized at that time, I had never given them enough information to defend themselves against such accusations.

Now, I begin my teaching by explaining that "reconcile" means to reestablish a relationship with one we have been separated from. Sin separates us from God. Reconciliation removes the sins that distance us from God. I explain what the words "confession" and "penance" mean and why we hear the sacrament referred to in these words. Then I go to the Bible and give them a full explanation of the sacrament they are preparing to receive. It's not a lesson I cover all at once—since they are still rather young—but just a little bit at a time.

Jesus began his ministry by calling for all to repent: "Repent, for the kingdom of heaven is at hand" (Mt 4: 17). Repenting means to change our ways, to reform our lives, to be sorry for our sins and to make up for our wrongdoings . That is why Jesus forgave sins throughout his ministry. We know forgiveness of sins is important. In John 8: 1–11, Luke 7: 48, and Mark 2: 10, there are examples of Jesus forgiving sins. He made healing of the body secondary to the healing of the soul. After curing a man who had been suffering for thirty-eight years, Jesus told him, "See, you are well! Sin no more, that nothing worse befall you" (Jn 5: 14).

Jesus gave the apostles the power to forgive sins. " . . . He breathed on them, and said to them, 'Receive the Holy Spirit. If you forgive the sins of any, they are forgiven; if you retain the sins of any, they are retained' " (Jn 20: 22–23). Just prior to giving his apostles the power to forgive sins, Jesus sent them out into the world to act in his place: "As the Father has sent me, even so I send you." Only God can forgive sins, but here he was giving them power which they were to use in his name.

Jesus bestowed this power on the apostles on Easter Sunday by breathing on them. In Genesis 2: 7 the Bible mentions God breathing on our first parents, when he breathed life into the first human beings. Likewise, through confession God breathes new life into our souls.

The apostles were given the authority to stand in for Jesus but it is he, Jesus, who forgives sins, not the priest. We confess our sins to Jesus through a priest . The priest acts in the place of Jesus when he administers the sacraments. He brings us closer to Jesus by acting as his representative, being physically present and able to forgive our sins in God's name and bring us instruction, encouragement and comfort. Confession is actually a meeting with Jesus and confessing our sins to him.

St. Paul explains how the Apostles are ambassadors of Christ's work of reconciliation:

> Therefore, if any one is in Christ, he is a new creation; the old has passed away, behold, the new has come. All this is from God, who through Christ reconciled us to himself and gave us the ministry of reconciliation; that is, God was in Christ reconciling the world to himself, not counting their trespasses against them, and entrusting to us the message of reconciliation. So we are ambassadors for Christ, God making his appeal through us (2 Cor 5: 17–20).

Also, Jesus told them: "Truly, I say to you, whatever you bind on earth shall be bound in heaven, and whatever you loose on earth shall be loosed in heaven" (Mt 18: 18). Only the apostles were told this, not the crowds that came to listen to Jesus. Jesus gave the apostles the power to bind and loose. Forgiving one's sins is loosing their sins. Jesus forgave sins during his time on earth and gave that power to the apostles for the time he would no longer be here. That power was subsequently passed on to keep the Church as Jesus established it, since the apostles would not always be on earth either. The power is from God.

Some Protestants teach that by accepting Jesus as our Savior we partake in the forgiveness of all our sins, past, present and future, based on his sacrifice on Calvary. But if God has already forgiven all man's sins, past and future, on the basis of a single act of repentance, then it makes no sense to tell the apostles they have been given the power to forgive or retain sins. It does, however, make sense that the Church, established by Jesus to perpetuate his work, would provide reconciliation of sinners by his appointed ministers.

> It follows . . . that the power of forgiving sins, on the part of God's minister, involves the obligation of confessing them on the part of the sinner. The Priest is not empowered to give absolution to everyone indiscriminately. He must exercise the power with judgment and discretion. He must reject the impenitent and absolve the penitent. But how will he judge of the disposition of the sinner unless he knows his sins, and how will the priest know his sins unless they are confessed? Hence, we are not surprised when we read in the Acts that "Many of them who

> believed came confessing and declaring their deeds" (Acts 19:18).[3]

The forgiveness we receive in confession is the first part of the sacrament. Forgiveness and the accompanying graces are what God brings us in the sacrament, but we also have our role. Of course we must be sorry for our sins and confess them first, but forgiveness does not erase the need to make up for the wrongdoing.

God forgave David for his adultery but his son died as temporal punishment for his sin (2 Sam 12:13–15). Moses was forgiven for striking the rock twice because he doubted, but still received temporal punishment; he was not allowed to lead the people into the Promised Land (Deut 34:4).

If we break a window or do damage, to simply say we are sorry and make no attempt to repair the wrong is seen as an imperfect apology. If we are truly sorry for what we have done we will want to atone, to make up for it in some way. Doing penance is a logical response on our part when we seek forgiveness.

During the Fourth Lateran Council in 1215, the Church prescribed that Catholics should confess their sins at least once a year. Some people point to this as evidence that the Church invented the sacrament at this time. Historical writings, however, show that the sacrament of Reconciliation was known and practiced in Christian communities in the early Church:

> From these extracts you can judge of the sentiments of all the Fathers on the subject of Confession. . . . St. Basil writes: "In the confession of sins the same method must be observed as in laying open the infirmities of the body; for as these are not rashly communicated to every one, but to those only who understand by what method they may be cured, so the confession of sins must be made to such persons as have the power to apply a remedy. . . . Necessarily, our sins must be confessed to those to whom has been committed the dispensation of the mysteries of God."

---

[3] James Cardinal Gibbons, *The Faith of our Fathers* (repr. Rockford, Ill.: Tan Books, 1980), p. 282.

> St. Ambrose, of Milan, writes: "The poison is sin; the remedy, the accusation of one's crime: the poison is iniquity; confession is the remedy of the relapse. . . ."
>
> St. Augustine writes: "Our merciful God wills us to confess in this world that we may not be confounded in the other." And again: "Let no one say to himself, I do penance to God in private, I do it before God. Is it then in vain that Christ hath said, 'Whatsoever thou shalt loose on earth shall be loosed in heaven?' Is it in vain that the keys have been given to the Church? Do we make void the Gospel, void the words of Christ?"
>
> St. John Chrysostom, in his thirtieth Homily, says: "Lo! we have now, at length, reached the close of Holy Lent; now especially we must press forward in the career of fasting . . . and exhibit a full and accurate confession of our sins . . . that with these good works, having come to the day of Easter, we may enjoy the bounty of the Lord. . . . For, as the enemy knows that having confessed our sins and shown our wounds to the physician we attain to an abundant cure, he in a special manner opposes us. . . . To cleanse the leprosy of the body, or rather to pronounce it cleansed, was given to the Jewish Priests alone. But to our Priest is granted the power not of declaring healed the leprosy of the body, but of absolutely cleansing the defilements of the soul."
>
> St. Jerome writes: "If the serpent, the devil, secretly bit a man and thus infected him with the poison of sin, and this man shall remain silent, and do no penance, nor be willing to make known his wound to his brother and master, the master, who has a tongue that can heal, cannot easily serve him. For if the ailing man be ashamed to open his case to the physician no cure can be expected; for medicine does not cure that of which it knows nothing."[4]

The last point I want to make about Confession is that if we want our children to receive the gift of Reconciliation on a regular basis, we need to go regularly ourselves.

[4] Ibid., pp. 283–285.

If you want a brief refresher course on Confession, the following is the New Rite of Penance:

Before going to Confession, make a thorough examination of conscience. Consider the commandments, especially the two Jesus gave us, to love God with our whole heart and soul and to love our neighbor as ourselves. Every time we put something between us and God, even the little things (not taking time to instruct our children properly on a religious issue, skipping prayers to watch TV, etc.) and any time we are not considerate of others, we have sinned.

The priest welcomes you. You make the sign of the cross, usually together with the priest. Begin your confession, "Bless me Father, for I have sinned. It has been (how long?) since my last confession. These are my sins: . . . Begin with any mortal sins, as these must be confessed. If one were to intentionally withhold a mortal sin out of embarrassment or whatever, he would be committing a grave sin, called a sacrilege, and the Confession would be invalid. Use a confessional with a screen or go to a church where the priest does not know you if it helps, but do not withhold a serious sin.

When you are done say: "For these and all the sins of my life I am sorry." Then, listen to any advice the priest gives you, and accept the penance he gives you to diminish the temporal punishment due to your sins. You then make an act of contrition; the priest usually asks you to do this. There are several wordings for an act of contrition. For example:

> *O my God, I am sorry for my sins. In choosing to sin and failing to do good, I have sinned against you and your Church. I firmly resolve, with the help of your grace to make up for my sins and to love as I should.*

Another form is:

> *O my God, I am heartily sorry for having offended you, and I detest all my sins because I dread the loss of heaven and the pains of hell; but most of all, because they offend you, my God, who are all-good and deserving of all my love. I firmly resolve, with the help of your grace, to confess my sins, to do penance, and to amend my life. Amen.*

The priest, then, acting in the person of Christ, forgives you your sins, saying the following words: "God, the Father of mercies, through the death and resurrection of his Son, has reconciled the world to himself and sent the Holy Spirit among us for the forgiveness of sins: through the ministry of the Church may God give you pardon and peace, and I absolve you from your sins, in the name of the Father, the Son, and the Holy Spirit" (as he makes the sign of the cross over you and you make the sign of the cross at the same time). The priest may say: "You may now go in peace to love and serve the Lord." You respond: "Thanks be to God," and then you say, "Thank you, Father."

If at any point you forget the format or get stuck, the priest will guide you along. This is not a test; so as long as you are truly sorry for your sins, you cannot flunk.

As a final note, you might wonder, if only Catholics have Confession, then are all people of other faiths who are guilty of mortal sin doomed to hell? The Church teaches (at the Council of Trent, 1551) that all people outside the Catholic Church must have perfect contrition in order to have their sins forgiven and grace restored, since most do not have the Sacrament of Reconciliation available to them. We, as Catholics, do have this gift; however, Jesus never forces his gifts on us. It is up to us to accept them by frequently making use of this wonderful sacrament, which is often called the sacrament of peace and of joy.

10

THE SACRAMENTS

Catholics recognize seven sacraments as being instituted by Christ and recorded in the Bible. It is yet another belief and practice that sets us apart from the other Christian denominations that do not believe in all seven. Because the sacraments of Penance and the Eucharist are available to us so frequently and offer such a bounty of grace and love into our lives, I have covered them in individual chapters.

The other five sacraments are also vitally important to our faith and should be understood. The sacraments, as we practice them, are often misunderstood by other denominations, so we should teach our children about them early on and explain why we believe they come from Christ.

The seven sacraments are: Baptism, Confirmation, Penance, Eucharist, Matrimony, Holy Orders, and the Anointing of the Sick. They are more than mere ceremonies or initiation rites. Sacraments are visible signs instituted by Christ by which grace is conveyed to our souls to bring us closer to God and help us on our journey to heaven. The *Catechism of the Catholic Church* explains:

> Seated at the right hand of the Father and pouring out the Holy Spirit on his Body which is the Church, Christ now acts through the sacraments he instituted to communicate his grace. The sacraments are perceptible signs (words and actions) accessible to our human nature. By the action of Christ and the power of the Holy Spirit they make present efficaciously the grace that they signify (CCC, no. 1084).

Baptism

Baptism is the first sacrament we would have received as Catholics. It is the gateway into the Catholic Church, because without it we may not receive the others. It may be the first encounter you or your children have in confronting different beliefs. It is also often the first conflict between spouses of different faiths.

Baptism, our Faith tells us, removes original sin—the deprivation of original holiness and justice—and fills us with sanctifying grace. We are reborn as children of God, and we receive the Holy Spirit into our soul. It gives life to our soul and makes it possible for us to enter into the kingdom of heaven. If the sacrament is received when one is an adult, it also removes all sin and any punishment due from those sins.

John the Baptist knew that Christ would bring the Holy Spirit to us through baptism. "I have baptized you with water; but he will baptize you with the Holy Spirit" (Mk 1:8).

The Catholic teaching is that the sooner a baby is baptized into Christ's Church, the better. "Now, why do you wait? Rise and be baptized, and wash away your sins, calling on his name" (Acts 22:16).

Christ commanded us:

> "Truly, truly, I say to you, unless one is born of water and the Spirit, he cannot enter the kingdom of God" (Jn 3:5).
>
> "Go therefore and make disciples of all nations, baptizing them in the name of the Father and of the Son and of the Holy Spirit" (Mt 28:19).
>
> And Peter said to them, "Repent and be baptized every one of you in the name of Jesus Christ for the forgiveness of your sins; and you shall receive the gift of the Holy Spirit. For the promise is to you and to your children and to all that are far off, every one whom the Lord our God calls to him" (Acts 2:38–39).

Although many Protestant denominations practice infant baptism, others believe children should not be baptized until the age of reason, when they can decide for themselves whether or not to be baptized. Many Protestants consider Baptism to be merely symbolic; the only real determination of salvation they feel is accepting Jesus Christ as your personal Lord and Savior.

The most common arguments against infant baptism are: (1) There is no such thing as original sin, and babies haven't sinned so they don't need baptism; (2) before the age of reason children aren't capable of making the choice to be baptized and they need to be mature enough to make the decision for themselves; (3) there are no examples of infant baptism in the Bible.

Let us begin with original sin, the sin we have inherited from Adam and Eve. "Therefore as sin came into the world through one man and death through sin, so death spread to all men because all men sinned . . ." (Rom 5: 12). Some will quibble over the translation, and say that this verse does not mean we have original sin. But please reread, "so death spread to all men because all men sinned."

In the Old Testament: "Can a man be found who is clean of defilement? There is none, however short his days" (Job 14: 4; NAB). In other words, even an infant ("however short his days") is not clean of defilement. Since an infant cannot sin, it must be original sin that is referred to.

The second argument, that children need to make this decision for themselves, is not consistent with other forms of good parenting. We have our children inoculated against infectious diseases, and give them medication if they become ill. We don't let our children run into the streets, or not bathe, or not go to school. We have to take care of their basic needs. Is filling their head with house rules and the ABC's more important than filling them with the Holy Spirit? Is bathing the outside of their body more important than purifying their soul?

We give our children what we consider important. If we don't have them baptized, we are saying in effect that it's not important. God wants us to be his children, and he gives children to their parents to raise. Parents should bring their children to God and not leave them without his saving grace. Yes, one day our children will have to make that choice for themselves. But in the meantime, it is entirely consistent with the authority God gives us over our children for us to choose God for them and to have them baptized.

It is more vital that we clothe our children in Christ than in the latest fashion. "For as many of you as were baptized into Christ have put on Christ" (Gal 3: 27).

As regards the third argument, that there are no examples of infant baptism in the Bible: first of all, not all revelation is contained in the Bible, as we explained earlier. There are two sources of revelation: Sacred Scripture and Sacred Tradition. There are plenty of examples of whole families, children included, being baptized in the writings of the early Fathers of the Church, and there are examples of children like St. Lucy, Sts. Felicity and Perpetua, and St. Agatha, being martyred at an early age for their faith. And besides, we also see whole households being baptized in Scripture, and a household usually contains children and babies. In the following passages there is no mention of children being excluded:

> And when she was baptized, with her household . . . (Acts 16: 15).
>
> He took them the same hour of the night, and washed their wounds, and he was baptized at once, with all his family (Acts 16: 33).
>
> I did baptize also the household of Stephanas. Beyond that, I do not know whether I baptized any one else (1 Cor 1: 16).

St. Paul noted that baptism replaces circumcision. Remember, circumcision was for infants, not for individuals reaching the age of reason. In the Old Testament, a child became part of the Old Covenant through circumcision, long before he could make his own decisions:

> God said to Abraham: . . . "Every male among you shall be circumcised. . . . He that is eight days old among you shall be circumcised" (Gen 17: 10, 12).
>
> In him also you were also circumcised with a circumcision made without hands, by putting off the body of flesh in the circumcision of Christ; and you were buried with him in baptism, in which you were also raised with him through faith in the working of God, who raised him from the dead (Col 2: 11–12).

There is some misunderstanding in regard to the importance of infant baptism because this principle leads some to the conclusion that babies and children dying without being baptized are doomed. But that is not what the Catholic Church teaches. We are taught to trust in God in this regard. The *Catechism* says:

> With respect to children who have died without Baptism, the liturgy of the Church invites us to trust in God's mercy and to pray for their salvation (CCC, no. 1283).

Confirmation

Jesus carried out his entire mission on earth in communion with the Holy Spirit. He was conceived of the Holy Spirit. The descent of the Holy Spirit at his baptism by John the Baptist was a sign that he was the Son of God, the long awaited Messiah. Jesus told the apostles he would give them the gift of the Holy Spirit:

> "For the Holy Spirit will teach you in that very hour what you ought to say" (Lk 12:12).

> "He who believes in me, as the scripture has said, 'Out of his heart shall flow rivers of living water.'" Now this he said about the Spirit, which those who believed in him were to receive (Jn 7:38–39).

> "Nevertheless I tell you the truth, it is to your advantage that I go away, for if I do not go away the Counselor will not come to you; but if I go, I will send him to you" (Jn 16:7).

> "But you shall receive power when the Holy Spirit has come upon you; and you shall be my witnesses in Jerusalem and in all Judea and Samaria and to the end of the earth" (Acts 1:8).

Christ fulfilled his promise to bring the Holy Spirit to his Apostles on Easter Sunday and then again on Pentecost.

> And when he had said this, he breathed on them, and said to them, "Receive the Holy Spirit" (Jn 20:22).

> And suddenly a sound came from heaven like the rush of a mighty wind, and it filled all the house where they were sitting. And there appeared to them tongues as of fire, distributed and resting on each one of them. And they

> were all filled with the Holy Spirit and began to speak in other tongues, as the Spirit gave them utterance (Acts 2:2–4).
>
> From that time on the apostles, in fulfillment of Christ's will, imparted to the newly baptized by the laying on of hands the gift of the Spirit that completes the grace of Baptism. For this reason in the Letter to the Hebrews the doctrine concerning Baptism and the laying on of hands is listed among the first elements of Christian instruction. The imposition of hands is rightly recognized by the Catholic tradition as the origin of . . . Confirmation, which in a certain way perpetuates the grace of Pentecost in the Church (Ap. Const. *Divinae Consortium Naturae*, no. 659).

Just as with infant baptism, some Christian denominations practice Confirmation while others do not recognize it as a sacrament. Catholics are supported by Scripture on this because the apostles prayed for and laid hands on the new converts, so the Holy Spirit would descend upon them:

> Now when the apostles at Jerusalem heard that Samaria had received the word of God, they sent to them Peter and John, who came down and prayed for them that they might receive the Holy Spirit; for it had not yet fallen on any of them, but they had only been baptized in the name of the Lord Jesus. Then they laid their hands on them and they received the Holy Spirit (Acts 8:14–17).
>
> And when Paul had laid his hands upon them the Holy Spirit came on them; and they spoke with tongues and prophesied (Acts 19:6).

The Holy Spirit fills us with grace to meet the spiritual challenges ahead. It continues the work of Baptism. And as with Baptism, Confirmation puts an indelible mark on our soul: ". . . he has put his seal upon us and given us his Spirit in our hearts as a guarantee" (2 Cor 1:22).

Children can easily understand that Confirmation continues the work of Baptism, filling us with the Holy Spirit, strengthening us for the work ahead as Christian soldiers to go out into the world and spread the message of Christ by word and example. During Confirmation, we also renew the baptismal promises, made for us by our parents (if we were very young children at the time of Baptism.) You can explain that, at Confirmation, they are now speaking for themselves and choosing to continue on the path they were placed on by their parents.

Older children preparing for Confirmation should be made familiar with all the Bible passages regarding this sacrament. It helps them understand the sacrament itself, and helps them prepare for it. Don't assume they are learning it at school or through religious program instruction because they might not be. And even if they are, it can't hurt to go over it at home, as parents should be the primary religious educators of their children.

Because children preparing for Confirmation are older, usually junior high age, many parents become less involved in teaching religion at this point. This is no time to let up. Be positive and cheerful. If they tune you out, try asking questions at the dinner table, or while driving in the car. For example, "Is Confirmation necessary to enter heaven?" (No), or "When was the first time the apostles received the Holy Spirit?" When I asked my two teenagers this second question, both answered: On Pentecost Sunday. The apostles received the fullness of the Holy Spirit on Pentecost Sunday, as Jesus promised, but on Easter Sunday Jesus said to them, "Receive the Holy Spirit," giving them the power to forgive sins. Try to make your children think, and get them involved.

It is good for them to know that Confirmation, like all the other teachings of the Church, is rooted in the Bible as well as in Tradition. The years ahead will likely present more challenges to their faith than the years behind did. It's definitely a great time for them to be receiving the Holy Spirit more fully. Help them to be open and ready to receive Him.

> "Behold, I send you out as sheep in the midst of wolves. . . . Beware of men; for they will deliver you up . . . and flog you . . . and you will be dragged before governors and kings for my sake, to bear testimony before them and the Gentiles. When they deliver you up, do not be anxious how you are to speak or what you are to say; for what you

> are to say will be given to you in that hour; for it is not you who speak, but the Spirit of your Father speaking through you" (Mt 10: 16–20).

Matrimony

Matrimony, or marriage, is the only sacrament administered by the two participants—the bride and groom—to each other. The priest officiates, but as a witness. The sacramental marriage bond is sacred and permanent.

> The sacrament of Matrimony signifies the union of Christ and the Church. It gives spouses the grace to love each other with the love with which Christ has loved his Church; the grace of the sacrament thus perfects the human love of the spouses, strengthens their indissoluble unity, and sanctifies them on the way to eternal life (cf. Council of Trent: *DS*, 1799) (CCC, no. 1661).

> Holy Scripture affirms that man and woman were created for one another: "It is not good that the man should be alone" [Gen 2: 18]. The woman, "flesh of his flesh," i.e., his counterpart, his equal, his nearest in all things, is given to him by God as a "helpmate"; she thus represents God from whom comes our help [Gen 2: 18]. "Therefore a man leaves his father and his mother and cleaves to his wife, and they become one flesh" [Gen 2: 24]. The Lord himself shows that this signifies an unbreakable union of their two lives by recalling what the plan of the Creator had been "in the beginning": "So they are no longer two, but one flesh" [Mt 19: 6] (CCC, no. 1605).

> This is a great mystery, and I mean in reference to Christ and the church; however, let each one of you love his wife as himself, and let the wife see that she respects her husband (Eph 5: 32–33).

> Be subject to one another out of reverence for Christ. Wives, be subject to your husbands, as to the Lord. For the husband is the head of the wife as Christ is the head of the church, his body, and is himself its Savior. As the

> church is subject to Christ, so let wives also be subject in everything to their husbands. Husbands, love your wives, as Christ loved the church and gave himself up for her, that he might sanctify her, having cleansed her by the washing of water with the word, that he might present the church to himself in splendor, without spot or wrinkle or any such thing, that she might be holy and without blemish. Even so husbands should love their wives as their own bodies. He who loves his wife loves himself (Eph 5:21–28).

I know the word "subject" angers some wives today, but I once heard a priest explain that husbands are given the heavier instruction: "Love your wives, as Christ loved the church." Christ died for his Church, and husbands likewise are to give totally of themselves to their spouse. We are told to be subject to one another. Christ came to serve, and he commands us to do the same. It was Satan who said, "I will not serve." Couples putting each other in such high regard will not be headed for divorce court.

It is true that the Old Testament records polygamy, but the exclusiveness of married love developed along with a deepened understanding of its unity and indissolubility, as seen in the books of Ruth and Tobit. The law as given to Moses did allow for divorce because of man's "hardness of heart" (Mt 19:8). But with the coming of Jesus, the Savior, many things changed, including a stricter teaching on the sacredness of marriage.

> And Pharisees came up and in order to test him asked, "Is it lawful for a man to divorce his wife?" He answered them, "What did Moses command you?" They said, "Moses allowed a man to write a certificate of divorce, and put her away." But Jesus said to them, "For your hardness of heart he wrote you this commandment. But from the beginning of creation, 'God made them male and female.' 'For this reason a man shall leave his father and mother and be joined to his wife, and the two shall become one.' So they are no longer two but one. What therefore God has joined together, let not man put asunder."
>
> And in the house the disciples asked him again about

> this matter. And he said to them, "Whoever divorces his wife and marries another, commits adultery against her; and if she divorces her husband and marries another, she commits adultery" (Mk 10:2–12).

> Thus a married woman is bound by law to her husband as long as he lives; but if her husband dies she is discharged from the law concerning her husband. Accordingly, she will be called an adulteress if she lives with another man while her husband is alive (Rom 7:2–3).

The Church does not teach spouses to stay in abusive, sinful, or morally damaging relationships. Also, the Church does grant annulments, but these are not the equivalent of divorces. An annulment determines that a true sacramental marriage never existed to begin with. A sacramental marriage is one between a baptized couple who freely consent to being married and understand what they are consenting to. There must not be ignorance in either spouse as to the nature and purpose of marriage; nor may there be deceit on either side. The spouses must not be under any coercion or grave external fear. If there had been ignorance or deceit at the time of the marriage, or if freedom was lacking, the marriage is not valid—there was no true marriage at all.

The Church's teaching on marriage was one of the trickiest things I had to explain during my five years as a fourth- and fifth-grade CCD teacher. The problem was that some children had divorced parents. The last thing I wanted to do was embarrass children or put them in the awkward position of judging their parents. Still, I could not compromise Church teaching.

Explain the Church's teaching on marriage clearly, noting that it can be difficult to follow. You can impress upon children that God has not put us in a position to judge. If we are concerned someone is not following the Church's teaching, we can pray for them and even talk to them about our concerns, but after that it is up to the couple, and we leave the matter to them and to God. Some couples remarried outside the Church eventually seek Church annulments and reenter the Church. We should never condemn individuals, but neither should we water down

Church teaching and think it does not hold in modern times. If some of you reading this book are not in compliance with Church teaching on marriage, you should talk about the matter with a priest and heed his recommendations.

> The remarriage of persons divorced from a living, lawful spouse contravenes the plan and law of God as taught by Christ. They are not separated from the Church, but they cannot receive Eucharistic communion. They will lead Christian lives especially by educating their children in the faith (CCC, no. 1665).

Divorce is common today, so many say the teachings of the Bible are out of date. Speaking from the experience of being a strong-willed person married to the same, I know marriage is not always bliss. Mark and I traveled a rocky road for a while, but because of our Catholic background, divorce was a step we were not willing to take. We personally discovered that marriage was not an outdated institution. Society's willingness (and thus the individual's) to end marriages is more a symptom of all the falling-away from Christian teachings than a failure of the institution of matrimony.

> This unequivocal insistence on the indissolubility of the marriage bond may have left some perplexed and could seem to be a demand impossible to realize. However, Jesus has not placed on spouses a burden impossible to bear, or too heavy, heavier than the Law of Moses (cf. Mk 8:34; Mt 11:29–30). By coming to restore the original order of creation disturbed by sin, he himself gives the strength and grace to live marriage in the new dimension of the Reign of God. It is by following Christ, renouncing themselves, and taking up their crosses that spouses will be able to "receive" the original meaning of marriage and live it with the help of Christ (cf. Mt 19:11). This grace of Christian marriage is a fruit of Christ's cross, the source of all Christian life (CCC, no. 1615).

The fact that marriages are in trouble is not the fault of the sacrament itself, but of our own failure to follow Christ: loving as we should, forgiving, praying together, and striving to live out the will of God. It's no coincidence that studies have shown a dramatically lower divorce rate among couples who attend church regularly together. The divorce rate among couples who regularly pray together is much lower again.

As Mark and I became better Catholics, our marriage improved. Through prayer, we received the help and graces we needed. When we try to do the will of God, we naturally make choices that also make us better spouses. You don't have to be Catholic to have a good marriage, but without Jesus in your relationship, it is certainly more difficult to overcome our selfishness each day and to be generous and self-giving to one's spouse and family.

Holy Orders

Through the sacrament of Holy Orders, the Catholic Church confers the priesthood on some chosen-by-God men. Other denominations teach that we are all called in some fashion to be priests but that is very different from Catholic Church teaching.

Some people say that Jesus told us to call no man "father" and yet we call our priests "father"—this, they say, is another example of how unbiblical Catholics are.

There is strong scriptural support, however, for the Catholic priesthood. Beginning with the Old Testament, we find that even though Israel was called to be a kingdom of priests, God still set aside certain men to serve as priests:

> You shall be to me a kingdom of priests and a holy nation (Ex 19:6).
>
> And also let the priests who come near to the Lord consecrate themselves . . . (Ex 19:22).
>
> And Melchizedek king of Salem brought out bread and wine; he was priest of God Most High. And he blessed [Abram] . . . (Gen 14:18–19).

The New Testament reiterates that we are all called to a general priesthood, as followers of Christ: "You are a chosen race, a royal priesthood, a holy nation, God's own people" (1 Pet 2:9).

Evangelizing was, and still is, the goal of all Christians, but

Scripture shows that certain men were specially chosen as ministers:

> While they were worshiping the Lord and fasting, the Holy Spirit said, "Set apart for me Barnabas and Saul for the work to which I have called them." Then after fasting and praying they laid their hands on them and sent them off (Acts 13:2–3).

St. Paul is one of these men called as a special minister, a priest:

> But on some points I have written to you very boldly by way of reminder, because of the grace given me by God to be a minister of Christ Jesus to the Gentiles in the priestly service of the gospel of God, so that the offering of the Gentiles may be acceptable, sanctified by the Holy Spirit (Rom 15:15–16).

The sacrament is conferred when a bishop lays his hands on and ordains men to the priesthood. Just as Jesus sent his first priests, the apostles, into the world, giving them special commands and powers, so today's priests are empowered to serve God in a ministerial role in his Church:

> These they set before the apostles, and they prayed and laid their hands upon them (Acts 6:6).
>
> Do not neglect the gift you have, which was given you by prophetic utterance when the elders laid their hands upon you (1 Tim 4:14).
>
> Hence I remind you to rekindle the gift of God that is within you through the laying on of my hands (2 Tim 1:6).

Once a man has been ordained a priest it is customary to call him "father." This practice is often used in an attempt to show the error in the Catholic priesthood because Scripture says that we should "call no man father."

> "But you are not to be called rabbi, for you have one teacher, and you are all brethren. And call no man your father on earth, for you have one Father, who is in heaven" (Mt 23:8–9).

In the above passage, Jesus was using a figure of speech to warn the Pharisees and scribes that they should not pridefully desire honorific titles. His words are not meant to be taken literally. The New Testament writers use "father" for natural fathers (Heb 12:7–11) and spiritual fathers in the Church (1 Cor 4:15; Philemon 10).

Jesus said there is but one teacher, yet we refer to educators as teachers all the time. Also, we call our biological dads "father." He was not telling us it was wrong to use these words, but that it is wrong to put a human in the seat of the Almighty, the ultimate Father and teacher. Jesus himself calls Abraham "father Abraham," in Luke 16:24.

St. Paul refers to himself as father. "For though you have countless guides in Christ, you do not have many fathers. For I became your father in Christ Jesus through the gospel" (1 Cor 4:15).

St. Stephen refers to his "fathers" in Acts 7:1–2, and the New Testament writers address men as father (see Rom 4:17–18; 1 Thess 2:11; 1 Jn 2:13–14.)

Priestly celibacy is also frequently attacked, but Christ's own example and Scripture recommend celibacy.

> ". . . and there are eunuchs who have made themselves eunuchs for the sake of the kingdom of heaven" (Mt 19:12).

> I want you to be free from anxieties. The unmarried man is anxious about the affairs of the Lord, how to please the Lord; but the married man is anxious about worldly affairs, how to please his wife, and his interests are divided. And the unmarried woman or girl is anxious about the affairs of the Lord, how to be holy in body and spirit; but the married woman is anxious about worldly affairs, how to please her husband. I say this for your own benefit, not to lay any restraint upon you, but to promote good order and to secure your undivided devotion to the Lord (1 Cor 7:32–35).

God blesses married life as holy, but those who feel called to a celibate single life for the love of God and his kingdom, are set aside in a special way to serve God. "So that he who marries his betrothed does well; and he who refrains from marriage will do better" (1 Cor 7:38).

I have a friend who was indignant over the whole Catholic priesthood. "It's ridiculous that they put such a burden as celibacy on men," she complained. Yet, I have heard several priests, who broke off engagements to enter the seminary, explain that while they were fighting the call to the priesthood, they lacked inner peace. Once they put their lives in God's hands and allowed themselves to investigate if God was truly calling them, it was then that they experienced fullness of joy.

I said to my friend, "I'm sure if people like you and me were in a religious order, we would be miserable because we are not called to that life. But those who have that vocation find true happiness in answering that call."

It is easy to see the advantages of a celibate priesthood. Anyone with a spouse and children knows the heavy responsibility they bring. An unmarried priest is free to give himself completely to God and to his spiritual flock. He is free to love God with all his heart and soul, to be very close to God and to bring others to God, and to bring God to others. There is no division of time between duties. It can all go to God and through him to the service of his people. He is also more available to go from one place to another according to the needs of the Church and the people, or even to move to another country. He does not have a wife and family to worry about.

It was during the fifth century that monasteries began to be organized for those wishing to give their lives totally to God as monks and nuns. They were characterized by the observance of what are known as the "evangelical counsels": poverty, chastity and obedience for the love of God. Countless schools, orphanages, hospitals and missions have been founded by those in a position to give themselves completely to God, to the Church and to the people of God.

Who can receive the Sacrament of Holy Orders?

"Only a baptized man (*vir*) validly receives sacred ordination" (*Code of Canon Law*, no. 1024). Why is that the case? Because that is what Jesus Christ established, and he is God. No power on earth can change what God has established.

We see women throughout the pages of the Gospel. Jesus always welcomed them and was courteous and helpful to them. Some women accompanied him as he journeyed with the Apostles through the towns and villages proclaiming the Good News of the Kingdom of God. These women provided for them out of their means. The Gospel names Joanna, who was the wife of Herod's steward, Susanna and "many others" (Lk 8: 1–3). "Jesus' words and works always express the respect and honor due to women" (John Paul II, *On the Dignity and Vocation of Women*, no. 13).

Yet Jesus chose men to be the twelve apostles and he only ordained men to the priesthood. The apostles did likewise, following his example and teaching.

People sometimes think of the Church and the priesthood in secular, human terms, as though it were some big business corporation or worldwide political organization. It is, in fact, a supernatural or divine organization, established by Jesus Christ himself. He laid down the basic principles and guidelines and these nobody can change. That is why the Church says in the *Catechism*: "The Church recognizes herself to be bound by this choice made by the Lord himself. For this reason the ordination of women is not possible" (CCC, no. 1577; cf. John Paul II, *Mulieris dignitatem*; CDF, *Inter insigniores*: AAS 69 [1977], 98–116).

Pope John Paul II frequently wrote and spoke about the dignity of women, made in the image and likeness of God and their equality with men. But the male-only priesthood has nothing to do with gender equality. It would be equally silly for men to complain because God didn't design them to have babies, as it would be for women to complain that he doesn't allow them to be priests. He is God after all, and he loves each of us wildly and he knows what is best for us and for the Church and the world.

Anointing of the Sick

The anointing of the sick is done as a way to channel grace to sick persons. It is intended to help them endure their suffering, in some cases to heal them, and to cleanse their souls and help them prepare to meet God.

A person who believes he is guaranteed heaven (is saved) simply by believing that Christ is his personal Lord and Savior may not see the point of this sacrament. However, the Bible instructs us on the value of the anointing of the sick:

> Is any among you sick? Let him call for the elders of the church, and let them pray over him, anointing him with oil in the name of the Lord; and the prayer of faith will save the sick man, and the Lord will raise him up; and if he has committed sins, he will be forgiven" (Jas 5:14–15.)

> And they cast out many demons, and anointed with oil many that were sick and healed them" (Mk 6:13).

The Catholic Church teaches that it was Jesus who gave us the seven sacraments. All seven sacraments began while Jesus was on earth. So what does this mean for non-Catholic Christians who have only two valid sacraments in their church? Fr. Fox explains it this way:

> It does *not* mean that Christians who lack the fullness of the sacraments are certainly lost, unless they knew the Catholic Church was the true Church of Jesus Christ himself with the fullness of truth and sacramental powers—and still refused to join it and partake of its services. Christians who lack the fullness of true faith but are sincere and do God's will as they understand it, may be saved if they are baptized and die with perfect contrition for any sins committed.[1]

[1] Fr. Robert J. Fox, *Covenant with Jesus* (New Hope, Ky.: Fatima Family Apostolate, 1996), p. 98.

11

OUR BLESSED MOTHER

Teaching your children about Mary, the Mother of Jesus and our Blessed Mother, gives a maternal dimension to our faith. God chose Mary to be the Mother of Jesus, his Son, from all eternity. She was an integral part of God's plan for our salvation. The annunciation was the time of fulfillment of God's promise to send a Messiah. Mary consented to her role in God's plan for man's salvation. The power of the Holy Spirit came upon Mary, causing her to conceive the eternal Son, Jesus Christ. His human nature is from her human nature.

Mary prompted Jesus to change the water into wine at the wedding feast of Cana. That was Christ's first public miracle. And Jesus gave us his Mother Mary to be our mother at the foot of the cross. Her earthly existence centered on bringing Jesus to us and now, if we go to her, she brings us closer to him.

God could have sent his Son any way he chose. He chose to go through Mary to come to us. If Mary is the way God chose to come to us, then she is certainly a good way for us to go to him. When we pray to Mary, we go to God with his chosen daughter, his virgin spouse and his Mother. When we honor her, we do as Jesus did when he followed the fourth commandment and honored his Mother. As God is our Father and Jesus is our Brother, then Mary completes the family as our Mother.

My own devotion to Mary began when I read about famous Church-endorsed apparitions of Mary at Lourdes and Fatima. It grew as I learned that many of our great saints turned to her as their mother in heaven. I started saying the rosary regularly and went to an occasional Catholic conference where speakers explained and commended the Church's tradition of honoring Mary.

As my own love for Mary grew, I became increasingly aware of the mixture of emotions she evokes: everything from love and devotion to aloofness and even discomfort. I've heard converted

Catholics admit that, in their former church, Mary was avoided. Mother's Day sermons might include every other woman in the Bible—Ruth, Sarah, Elizabeth—but nary a word about Mary, the mother of our Lord and Savior. I once heard a speaker tell of witnessing another speaker kick a statue of Mary to demonstrate that she had no place in our relationship with God. Granted, this is an extreme example, but outside the Catholic Church there is a lot of discomfort when it comes to having a relationship with Mary, the Blessed Mother.

Many non-Catholics feel that praying to Mary borders on idolatry. People say she is a mere human and should not be elevated in any way. They think it is preposterous to claim she was conceived without original sin, remained a virgin, is the Mother of God, and ascended into heaven in body and soul. Even some Catholics make a point of avoiding any sort of Marian devotion. Instead, they consider Mary non-essential to religion. They fail to see that Mary illuminates faith in Christ.

If we want our children to find comfort and heavenly aid through the Blessed Mother, we should help them understand the basis for the Catholic tradition of honoring Mary as the Mother of our Savior. There are several arguments against a devotion to Mary. I will list them here and then tackle each individually. First, some denominations believe that we simply cannot communicate with Mary, or any of the saints for that matter. And, even if we could communicate with her, some say the Bible speaks against using her, or the saints, as intermediaries. Those that avoid Mary say there is no evidence that Mary was conceived without sin (the doctrine known as the Immaculate Conception) or was "ever-virgin" or assumed into heaven (the Assumption) body and soul. And lastly, even if all the above were true, many non-Catholic Christian denominations hold that there is no biblical basis for devotion to Mary.

Let us begin by asking, how can we know that Mary hears us if we pray to her? Some people believe that those in heaven are praying for us, but we cannot communicate personally with them. This belief contends that contact between those who have gone before us and those still on earth is not possible. Consider the logic here. Some of the same people that believe that the devil influences our lives through temptation are saying that

God would give the devil the ability to communicate through the spiritual realm, but not his own Mother.

Catholics believe that as "one body" in Christ, there is no separation between us and those in heaven and that they can hear our prayers to them. For a biblical example, look at the Transfiguration (Lk 9:28–36), when Moses and Elijah appeared with Jesus before Peter, James, and John. This passage offers biblical evidence that there is not an impenetrable wall between heaven and earth.

As long as we are considering this example, also note that Peter suggested erecting tents for Jesus, Moses, and Elijah, right there on the mountaintop. He wanted to honor them. Moses and Elijah were special people with special relationships with God. Honoring them was not idolatry, it was a natural reaction—honoring holy ones who have gone before us. By honoring them, we honor God. All that is worth honoring is only that which reflects the goodness of God. Mary especially reflects this because she was God's chosen instrument to work with her Son as he wrought the salvation of mankind.

Now let us ask the next question: even if Mary can hear us, doesn't the Bible teach against going to God through anyone but Jesus?

According to 1 Timothy 2:5, there is only one mediator between God and man—Jesus. People use this verse to claim there is no mediator but Jesus, so we cannot go through Mary. Yet, these same people believe that our friends here on earth can pray for us. If the prayers of our friends help, what better friend and helper could we have than the Mother of Jesus? St. Paul made it clear that prayers can be said for others:

> First of all, then, I urge that supplications, prayers, intercessions, and thanksgivings be made for all men, for kings and all who are in high positions, that we may lead a quiet and peaceable life, godly and respectful in every way. This is good and it is acceptable in the sight of God our Savior . . . (1 Tim 2:1–3).

> You also must help us by prayer, so that many will give thanks on our behalf for the blessing granted us in answer to many prayers (2 Cor 1:11).

When we go to Mary, we ask her to help us with her prayers. The Bible tells us how close she was to her Son. A good word put in by Mary proved to be quite effective at the wedding at Cana:

> When the wine failed, the mother of Jesus said to him, "They have no wine." And Jesus said to her, "O woman, what have you to do with me? My hour has not yet come." His mother said to the servants, "Do whatever he tells you" (Jn 2:3–5).

I heard a priest once point out that he had been to a lot of weddings but he'd never been to one where the guests drank all the wine. "This wasn't even a good miracle," he claimed. "To top it off, Jesus plainly said it was not his time. Yet, his mother's intervention moved him to perform his first recorded miracle." As the priest explained, he did it for one reason—because his Mother asked him.

A Protestant friend once argued with me, "But it was his time or he would not have done it." I prefer to take Jesus at his word, and he plainly said it was not his time. He made it his time in order to respond to his Mother, and it was recorded in the Bible as such. Surely there was a divine plan Jesus followed from the start, and there must have been a reason his first miracle was performed at the request of his Mother. The miracle clearly shows the effectiveness of Mary's intervention. It was her intervention that began his public ministry and her words on that occasion lead us to her Son: "Do whatever he tells you."

The arguments against Mary being "ever virgin" use the Bible to claim she had other children. One argument is that, in Luke 2:7, Jesus is described as the "first-born," and so there must have been at least a second-born. But "first-born" was a ceremonial title given to the first-born male child, who inherited a unique birthright from his father (Gen 25:33) and even only children held this title.

Also, the passage that he "knew her not until she had borne a son; and he called his name Jesus" (Mt 1:25) is misinterpreted. Some focus on the word "until," held to mean the same as we tend to use it in English: it was this way *until* some other event happened. Just look a little further in your Bible to 1 Corinthians 15:25, where it says Christ must reign "until" he has put all enemies beneath his feet. That doesn't mean his reign will cease then. Then look back in 2 Samuel 6:23. King David's wife is said to have had "no child to the day of her death." The word "to" certainly doesn't mean that after her death, things changed.

And finally, a third scriptural argument is where Matthew 13:55 lists Jesus' brothers as James, Joseph, Simon, and Judas, proof, I have been told, that Mary was not "ever-virgin." But the Hebrew and Aramaic languages, the languages used by Christ, did not have separate words for brothers, cousins, and near-relatives. Luke 6:15–16 reveals that James, though elsewhere called the brother of Jesus, was the son of Alphaeus. No one else but Jesus, including those referred to as his brethren, is ever referred to as a son of Mary. In Mark 6:3, Jesus is called "the son of Mary," not "one of the sons of Mary."

The other difficult points for those with an aversion to honoring Mary are the Catholic beliefs that Mary was conceived without original sin on her soul (known as the "Immaculate Conception") and the belief that Mary was assumed body and soul into heaven (the Assumption). Remember, God chose Mary to be the mother of his Son, Jesus. Would God have chosen to have his only begotten Son become flesh in a body that was subject to Satan if it were possible otherwise? How unfitting it would have been to have Jesus grow in a womb that bore the stain of original sin.

Bring "a clean vessel to the house of the Lord" (Is 66:20). Vessels used in church services were set apart by special consecration, how much more would Mary be set apart, the chosen vessel of our Lord?

Some reject this teaching because they reason that if Mary was conceived without original sin, then somehow or other she did not descend from our first parents, Adam and Eve, because, as she did not inherit original sin, she did not need a savior. The Catholic teaching is that Mary was indeed saved by Christ. "My spirit rejoices in God my Savior" (Lk 1:47). At the moment of her conception Mary was preserved from original sin through the anticipated merits of her Son's death. She was saved in advance through the merits of Christ's passion, death, and resurrection.

Also, Romans 3:23 seems to indict Mary as a sinner like the rest of us: "All have sinned and fall short of the glory of God." We must be careful not to take one word, "all," and misconstrue the point St. Paul is making. He is stressing the universal aspect of sin, stating that this includes both Jews and Gentiles alike. He is speaking in general terms. St. Paul is stating a general principle, not mentioning exceptions.

It is surprising and not very logical that many people who believe Enoch and Elijah were assumed into heaven refuse to believe that Jesus did the same for his own mother:

> Then Enoch walked with God; and he was not, for God took him (Gen 5:24).

> By faith Enoch was taken up so that he should not see death; and he was not found, because God had taken him (Heb 11:5).

> As they still went on and talked, behold, a chariot of fire and horses of fire separated the two of them. And Elijah went up by a whirlwind into heaven (2 Kings 2:11).

During the early years of the Church, the bones of saints were kept and highly regarded as relics. No church ever claimed the bones of Mary. Certainly, if Mary had not been assumed into heaven, members of the Church would have treasured and guarded her bones. We also rely on sacred Tradition, which held this belief from earliest times.

Remember, the sacred vessels of the church were set aside for special consecration. Consider the improbability that Mary, the first tabernacle of Christ, with a womb that held God, would have been allowed to decay in the ground.

Accusations have been made that the Catholic Church simply made these two teachings up in modern times. This is a misunderstanding of the fact that the Catholic Church officially defined the already existing doctrines of the Immaculate Conception in 1854 and the Assumption in 1950. At certain times the Church chooses to codify a belief that has always existed either because the Pope sees a benefit to the Church by infallibly defining and proclaiming an already well-established belief, or because there arises a need to defend it against confusion or attack. Both these beliefs existed since the early Church and were not made up in modern times. As infallibly defined dogmas of faith, acceptance of these two teachings is required of all Catholics. The Protestant belief in *sola scriptura* prevents many from accepting these two teachings on Mary, but nowhere does Scripture refute them.

Even if you could convince someone of the possibility that Mary remained a virgin, was conceived without sin, and was assumed body and soul into heaven they might still insist that there is no biblical basis for the Catholic Church to elevate Mary above the rest of mankind. That argument used to trouble me. I could counter that it was a historically Christian thing to do because the early Church practiced devotion to Mary. She was, of course, present on all the important occasions: Jesus' birth, Presentation, first miracle, crucifixion, Ascension, and with the apostles on Pentecost Sunday. And it is likely that her input provided the information for the beginning of the Gospels of Luke and Matthew, so she was certainly an important person to the Church.

But, if you have ever had a debate with a "show me where it says that in the Bible," kind of person, your only hope of making points is actually to find it in the Bible. So, I was very pleased when I discovered that the Catholic custom of honoring Mary is completely biblical. The queenship of Mary and the tradition of honoring and going to the queen for intercession is a tradition rooted in the Old Testament. I'm going to borrow heavily from a magazine article that says it far better than I could:

> In the monarchy of King David, as well as in other ancient kingdoms of the Near East, the mother of the ruling king held an important office in the royal court and played a key part in the process of dynastic succession. In fact the king's mother ruled as queen, not his wife. [Remember, back then the kings often had several wives, making their queenship next to impossible.]
>
> A number of Old Testament passages reflect the important role of the queen mother in the Davidic kingdom. For example, almost every time the narrative of 1 and 2 Kings introduces a new monarch in Judah, it mentions the king's mother, as well, showing the mother's intimate involvement in her royal son's reign. . . .

> Her royal office is also described by the prophet Jeremiah, who tells how the queen mother possessed a throne and a crown, symbolic of her position of authority in the kingdom . . . (Jer 13: 18, 20).
>
> Probably the clearest example of the queen mother's role is that of Bathsheba, wife of David and mother of Solomon . . . after her son Solomon assumed the throne and she became queen mother, Bathsheba receives a glorious reception upon meeting with her royal son.
>
> So Bathsheba went to King Solomon, to speak to him on behalf of Adonijah. And the king rose to meet her, and bowed down to her; then he sat on his throne and had a seat brought for the king's mother; and she sat on his right. Then she said, "I have one small request to make of you; do not refuse me." And the king said to her, "Make your request, my mother; for I will not refuse you" (1 Kings 2: 19–20).[1]

In the Bible, the right hand is the place of highest honor (e.g. Ps 110; Heb 1: 13), so the queen sitting at the king's right hand symbolizes sharing in the king's authority and illustrates that she is second only to the king himself. Isaiah 9: 6–7 and 11:1–2 are among the Old Testament prophecies that link the kingship of David with the future messianic king. Also, "Hear then, O house of David! Is it too little for you to weary men, that you weary my God also? Therefore the Lord himself will give you a sign. Behold, a young woman shall conceive and bear a son and shall call his name Immanuel" (Is 7: 13–14). Then, in the New Testament, Matthew 1: 23 refers to this prophecy as being fulfilled in Jesus.

> Since the oracle is addressed specifically to the Davidic household and concerns the continuation of the dynasty, the young woman bearing forth the royal son would be understood as a queen mother. This has implications for our understanding of Mary. Since the mother of the king always ruled as queen mother, we should expect to find

[1] Edward P. Sri, "Is Mary's Queenship Biblical?" *This Rock* (December 1998), pp. 15–16.

> the mother of the messianic king playing the role of the true queen mother in the everlasting Kingdom of God.
>
> . . . Matthew emphasizes that Jesus is "the Son of David," who is the true King of the Jews establishing the "Kingdom of Heaven." With all this kingly imagery, it should not be surprising to find queen mother themes as well.
>
> . . . Just as the queen mother was constantly mentioned alongside the Judean kings in 1 and 2 Kings, so Mary is frequently mentioned alongside her royal son, Jesus, in Matthew's infancy narrative (Mt 1:18; 2:11, 13, 14, 20, 21).[2]

Luke's Gospel also shows strong links to the kingdom of David. For instance, the angel Gabriel appeared to a virgin betrothed to a man, "of the house of David" (1:27). Again in Luke 1:32–33, the angel tells Mary her son will be great, called Son of the Most High, "And the Lord God will give to him the throne of his father David, and he will reign over the house of Jacob for ever; and of his kingdom there will be no end."

> Mary's royal office is made even more explicit in Luke's account of the Visitation. Elizabeth greets Mary with the title 'the mother of my Lord' (Lk 1:43). This title is charged with great queenly significance. In the royal court language of the ancient Near East, the title "Mother of my lord" was used to address the queen mother of the reigning king (who himself was addressed as "my lord"; cf. 2 Sam 24:21). Thus with this title Elizabeth is recognizing the great dignity of Mary's role as the royal mother of the king, Jesus.
>
> Finally, Mary's queenship can be seen in the great vision described in Revelation 12: "And a great portend appeared in heaven, a woman clothed with the sun, with the moon under her feet and on her head a crown of twelve stars; she was with child and she cried out in her pangs of birth, in anguish for delivery" (Rev 12:1–2). Who is this

[2] Ibid., pp. 16–17.

> newborn child? He is described as the messianic king exercising his dominion. In verse 5, the author of Revelation chose the messianic Psalm 2 to describe how this child will "rule all the nations with a rod of iron" (Rev 12:5, Ps 2:9). This royal son is taken up to heaven to sit on a throne (Rev 12:5) and he ushers in the kingdom of God by defeating the devil; "Now the kingdom of our God has come, for the accuser has been thrown down" (Rev 12:10). Certainly, this newborn child is the royal Messiah, King Jesus.[3]

The arguments offered in the article quoted above may be too complicated for children, but since Mary's queenship is so often attacked as unbiblical, I wanted to include a full explanation for parents. However, I explained it to my children quite simply: During the time of David, the queen mother played an important role and was honored along with her son. It was to the queen mother whom the people went with their petitions to be brought to her son, the king. Therefore, keeping in mind that Jesus descended from the house of David and the Bible repeatedly brings out the strong connection, Catholics are merely following the tradition already established and clearly laid out in the Bible.

The most important single fact is that Jesus Christ is God, and that Mary is the Mother of Christ. Hence, Mary is the Mother of God. All her privileges follow as a consequence—her Immaculate Conception, her perpetual virginity, her bodily assumption into heaven, her mediation between God and man. And because she is the Mother of God, we love, respect and venerate her in a very special way.

A number of Catholic practices relating to Mary are also Biblically based, for instance, the Hail Mary. "Hail, full of grace, the Lord is with you" (Lk 1:28); "Blessed are you among women, and blessed is the fruit of your womb!" (v. 42). The next part, "Holy Mary" comes from, "you have found favor with God" (v. 30) and "Mother of God" comes from "mother of my Lord" (v. 43). The rest, "Pray for us sinners now and at the hour of our death. Amen," is a request to Mary to pray for us.

---

[3] Ibid., p. 17.

Surprisingly, devotion to Mary was once acceptable for Protestants. Anyone reviewing the writings of some of the more important leaders of the Reformation can clearly see that, in spite of major disagreement with Catholic teachings, they shared a strong devotion to Mary. You may be surprised by the affirmation of some very Catholic beliefs about Mary being put forth by leaders in the Reformation:

> Luther, Calvin, and Zwingli, the three fathers of the Reformation, each affirmed the Catholic doctrines that Mary is the Mother of God and a Perpetual Virgin.
>
> *Mary as Mother of God:*
>
> Martin Luther: "In this work whereby she was made the Mother of God, so many and such good things were given her that no one can grasp them. . . . Not only was Mary the mother of him who is born (in Bethlehem), but of him who, before the world, was eternally born of the Father, from a Mother in time at the same time man and God" (Weimer, *The Works of Luther*, trans. by Pelikan, Concordia, St. Louis, v. 7, p. 572).
>
> John Calvin: "It cannot be denied that God in choosing and destining Mary to be the Mother of his Son, granted her the highest honor. . . . Elizabeth calls Mary, Mother of the Lord, because the unity of the person in the two natures of Christ was such that she could have said that the mortal man engendered in the womb of Mary was at the same time the eternal God" (*Calvin Opera, Corpus Reformatorum*, Braunschweig-Berlin, 1863–1900, v. 45, pp. 348, 35).
>
> Ulrich Zwingli: "It was given to her what belongs to no creature, that in the flesh she should bring forth the Son of God" (*Zwingli Opera, Corpus Reformatorum*, Berlin, 1905, in Evang. Luc., Op. comp., v. 6, I, p. 639).
>
> *Mary as Perpetual Virgin*
>
> Luther: "It is an article of faith that Mary is Mother of the Lord and still a virgin. . . . Christ, we believe, came forth from a womb left perfectly intact" (*Works of Luther*, v. 11, pp. 319–20; v. 6, p. 510).

> Calvin: "There have been certain folk who have wished to suggest from this passage (Mt 1:25) that the Virgin Mary had other children than the Son of God, and that Joseph had then dwelt with her later; but what folly this is! For the gospel writer did not wish to record what happened afterwards; he simply wished to make clear Joseph's obedience and to show also that Joseph had been well and truly assured that it was God who had sent his angel to Mary. He had therefore never dwelt with her nor had he shared her company. . . . And besides this Our Lord Jesus Christ is called the first-born. This is not because there was a second or a third, but because the gospel writer is paying regard to the precedence. Scripture speaks thus of naming the first-born whether or no there was any question of the second" (*Sermon on Matthew* 1:22–25, published 1562).
>
> Zwingli: "I firmly believe that Mary, according to the words of the gospel, as a pure Virgin brought forth for us the Son of God and in childbirth and after childbirth forever remained a pure, intact Virgin" (*Zwingli Opera*, v. 1, p. 424).[4]

Catholics continue the devotion to Mary that was present at the time of the Reformation. By honoring Mary, Catholics fulfill Luke 1:48–49, "All generations will call me blessed." We unabashedly call Mary our Blessed Mother. It was not Catholics who began a devotion to Mary. God is the one who heaped unequaled honor on a mere human being by inviting her to be the Mother of God. We are redeemed by the blood of her Son. Jesus became flesh and blood of her flesh and blood. Our earthly mother gives us life, while Mary, our heavenly Mother gave us supernatural life by consenting to the plan God laid before her, to give birth to our Savior and in turn bring him to us. She gave birth to Jesus for our salvation. Jesus, our brother, told us to follow Him. If God has so honored Mary as the daughter of God the Father, Mother of God the Son, and spouse of God the Holy

[4] Fr. Frank Chacon and Jim Burnham, *Beginning Apologetics I* (San Juan Catholic Seminars, 1993), p. 20.

Spirit, how could we do otherwise? We are following him by honoring Mary.

We look with reverence on everyone and everything associated with Jesus Christ. People make trips to the Holy Land in droves for this very reason; to walk on the same land Jesus once walked on. If lifeless soil is such an attraction, how much more should we hold in esteem the living souls of those closely associated with Jesus? And who could have been closer to him than his own Mother? She carried him in her womb, nursed and clothed Him, guided his first steps and cared for him into adulthood.

We build monuments to great people of much lesser stature than Mary (e.g., the Washington monument, the Lincoln Memorial, schools, streets, holidays). By honoring a great American, do we dishonor God? Of course not. Anyone with qualms about honoring Mary should consider these inconsistencies. Remember, we honor Mary, we do not worship her. Her goodness is only a reflection of God's greatness.

One last aspect regarding the Blessed Mother that has not been brought up thus far: the many apparitions and messages of the Blessed Mother that have been reported throughout the history of the Church. I do not include this in the main argument because it is not required of Catholics to believe in any apparition of Mary. The Church itself is very slow and conservative about giving a nod of approval to any claim of Mary appearing on earth. After much investigation, the Church does sometimes acknowledge that such a supernatural event is worthy of belief. Many miracles and conversions often result through these apparitions, and many such sites have been visited by millions of Pilgrims, such as those at Fatima, Portugal, Lourdes, France, and the shrine of Our Lady of Guadalupe in Mexico.

Pope Urban VIII stated his opinion that, "In cases like this, it is better to believe than not to believe, for if you believe and it is proven true, you will be happy that you have believed because our holy Mother asked it. If you believe and it should be proven false, you will receive all blessings as if it had been true, because you believed it to be true." However, in cases where the visions contradict Church teaching and are condemned by the Church as false, and not from God, they should clearly be avoided.

12

FAITH AND WORKS

A major difference between Catholics and many of our Protestant friends is the question of how we are saved. We share a confidence that Jesus' death on the cross saved us all from sin and death so that one day we can enjoy eternal happiness with him in heaven. That's a big point of agreement. Yet, our different views on how God allows us to be saved opens up an ecumenical chasm.

Protestants believe that "faith alone" is all you need. They teach that if you believe in the Lord Jesus Christ as your personal Lord and Savior your salvation is guaranteed from that point on. Once you believe, the job is done. You live your life out, naturally wanting to please God, but, regardless of failings, the first thing you will see after your last breath will be heaven. Once you have faith, the teaching goes, works may follow according to a natural desire, but you need not worry because you've done your part to get into heaven if you believe in Jesus Christ. This is a one-time act that offers absolute salvation.

Catholics are often accused of trying to be saved through our good works, but in fact we also believe we are saved by our faith. The difference, however, is that traditional Protestant teaching says "faith alone," while Catholics say faith is only the beginning. We believe that faith will express itself in good works if it is lived out, while Protestants believe if there is faith, works do not matter because we are saved. The Catholic interpretation of salvation puts some of the responsibility on our shoulders. Protestants often mistakenly interpret that to mean Catholics think we are saving ourselves with works. We know that alone we are helpless to save ourselves. The Church teaches that nobody is justified by works alone. We are saved by our Lord's passion, death and resurrection. It is our faith in Christ's redeeming merits that saves us, along with our good works in response to that faith. Our good works protect our faith and are the necessary response. Catholics believe that nobody's salvation is guaranteed. But if we use all the means available to us in the Church, frequenting the sacraments and striving to live our lives as God wants to the end, we believe that God in his goodness and mercy will welcome us into heaven.

Father Chacon and Jim Burnham give this explanation:

> We agree with Protestants that the redemptive work of Christ is complete and all-sufficient. Through his suffering, death, and resurrection, Jesus redeemed everyone; he paid for all sins and made it possible for anyone to be saved. However, we know that not everyone is automatically saved.
>
> All Christians admit that people can fail to be saved by refusing to repent, or by refusing to cooperate with God's grace in other areas. Although the redemptive work of Christ is complete, the merits of his redemption must still be applied to each person in order for him to be saved. Thus, a person must repent (Mt 4:17), believe in Jesus (Acts 16:31), keep the commandments (Mt 19:16–17), and live a life of charity (1 Cor 13:1–3), as Scripture plainly teaches. A Catholic who performs good works in Christ isn't denying the fullness of Christ's redemption; he is depending on it.[1]

The differences in these beliefs results in differences in how we teach our children to follow their faith. A child believing that "faith alone" is all that is required will obviously approach life in a different way from someone who feels a personal responsibility to serve God as a follow-up to his or her faith.

My son Luke, reflecting on this, once commented, "If they were right, it would sure make things a lot easier." The Bible, however, repeatedly tells us in so many places that it takes effort to fully live our faith. My son believes that God expects more from us than just faith. He chuckled and said, "I know. But it sure would be an easy way to get to heaven."

This is actually a simple lesson for children to understand.

---

[1] Fr. Frank Chacon and Jim Burnham, *Beginning Apologetics I* (San Juan Catholic Seminars, 1993), p. 37.

Point out that our salvation is a gift from Jesus and it begins with our faith in Him. Then, read Bible passages, like the many I have used in this chapter, to show that the Bible teaches we can lose salvation and also that Jesus told us in many ways how we are to follow him. If your children are young, rather than get bogged down in endless passages, the two commandments given by Jesus encompass what it means to follow Christ and live our faith.

> The first is, "Hear, O Israel: The Lord our God, the Lord is one; and you shall love the Lord your God with all your heart, and with all your soul, and with all your mind, and with all your strength." The second is this, "You shall love your neighbor as yourself" (Mk 12:29–31).

That is a very high standard to live up to, and it takes real effort on our part to do so. We must make the effort day in and day out. Loving God means nothing if we do not know, love, and serve him all the way. And how can we say we love our neighbors if we do not do things for them?

To teach this lesson to older children, you can show them the Bible passages that support a belief in salvation by "faith alone." Then you can look at all the instructions God gave us through Scripture that supports the belief that works are necessary for our salvation and that salvation can be lost. You could sit down with your children and cover this as an actual lesson, but I prefer to do it little by little. When we read the Bible together and come across passages that say we are saved by faith, I point out that this is where the Protestant belief of "faith alone" came from. I explain that this teaching was unheard of before the Protestant Reformation. (The word "alone" does not appear in the Bible in the original Greek text, but was put in later Protestant versions by Martin Luther to make the teaching clear according to his way of thinking.) Likewise, I bring to their attention the Bible verses that give clear commands for works—responsibility involving our personal effort. I also point out the Scripture passages that tell us salvation can be lost—that it is not guaranteed by faith alone. I've provided a number of examples of these passages below, beginning with the basis for the Protestant belief:

> They are justified by his grace as a gift, through the redemption which is in Christ Jesus, whom God put forward as an expiation by his blood, to be received by faith. This was to show God's righteousness, because in his divine forbearance he had passed over former sins; it was to prove at the present time that he himself is righteous and that he justifies him who has faith in Jesus (Rom 3:24–26).

> For we hold that a man is justified by faith apart from works of law (Rom 3:28).

In these passages, St. Paul is teaching that the works of the Old Testament Mosaic law, for example, circumcision, did not bring salvation. Catholics agree that without the grace afforded us through Jesus and without faith, we will be lost. The difference is we believe there is still one more step toward salvation that we must take:

> But by the grace of God I am what I am, and his grace toward me was not in vain. On the contrary, I worked harder than any of them; though it was not I, but the grace of God which is with me (1 Cor 15:10).

> For by grace you have been saved through faith, and this is not you own doing; it is the gift of God—not because of works, lest any man should boast" (Eph 2:8–9).

Catholics believe our faith begins with grace and it is a free gift from God. There are sanctifying grace and actual grace. Actual grace is God's push toward faith in Him. Sanctifying grace raises a soul so it is capable of heaven. We lose sanctifying grace through mortal sin and regain it through Confession, and increase it through the sacraments. Nothing unclean can enter heaven, therefore, we can lose heaven through our sin.

Another Bible passage Protestants use to claim salvation is by faith is: "My sheep hear my voice, and I know them, and they follow me; and I give them eternal life, and they shall never perish, and no one shall snatch them out of my hand" (Jn 10:27–29).

We agree the gift of eternal life comes from Jesus. We also agree that no one can take that from us. That does not mean that we ourselves cannot turn from Jesus' voice and choose to leave his protective hand. He is merely saying outside forces cannot take away our salvation.

> For I through the law died to the law, that I might live to God. I have been crucified with Christ; it is no longer I who live, but Christ who lives in me; and the life I now live in the flesh I live by faith in the Son of God, who loved me and gave himself for me. I do not nullify the grace of God; for if justification were through the law, then Christ died to no purpose (Gal 2: 19–21).

Yes, Jesus saved us with his love through his death on the cross, not by the [Old Testament] law, so we follow Christ by following his instructions on how to live a holy life. We agree that salvation is a free gift, bought for us through the sacrifice of Jesus. We cannot earn it for ourselves, but we use free will to accept this gift by choosing to follow Christ—every moment of our lives, with every choice we make. To believe in Christ and choose salvation means we must follow him and obey him. We believe that, rather than a one-time decision, we must choose Christ daily, and many times a day, and that we are capable of turning away from him, of losing our faith and thus our salvation:

> Therefore, since we are justified by faith, we have peace with God through our Lord Jesus Christ. Through him we have obtained access to this grace in which we stand, and we rejoice in our hope of sharing the glory of God (Rom 5: 1–2).

> For in this hope we were saved (Rom 8: 24).

Both these passages say “in hope,” not “in assurance.” Catholics have hope in their salvation, not assurance.

Let us look at some Scripture passages that show that “faith alone” is not enough:

> What does it profit, my brethren, if a man says he has faith but has not works? Can his faith save him?” (Jas 2: 14).

> Show me your faith apart from your works, and I by my works will show you my faith. . . . For as the body apart

> from the spirit is dead, so faith apart from works is dead (Jas 2:18, 26).

Luther and other Protestants exclude St. James' Letter from the New Testament altogether, largely because it undermines their theory that we are saved by faith alone and that good deeds are not required. Other, less radical, Protestants explain these words of James by saying that, with faith, works naturally follow. They believe that if there are no works then that shows there is no faith. But James is talking about faith with works as opposed to faith without works, not faith and non-faith. A person without works, according to Protestant teaching, would be lacking in faith. But that is not what James says. He has confined his topic to people of faith—those who perform works and those who do not.

St. Paul says faith alone is not enough: ". . . if I have all faith, so as to remove mountains, but have not love, I am nothing" (1 Cor 13:2). Remember, even the devil believes in Jesus. He has no doubt of Jesus' existence, but he has no love.

At the Last Supper Jesus explained how important love is. "He who has my commandments and keeps them, he it is who loves me; and he who loves me will be loved by my Father, and I will love him and manifest myself to him" (Jn 14:21).

When a rich man asked Jesus what he had to do to gain eternal life, Jesus did not say to believe in him as the man's personal Lord and Savior. He gave him instructions. ". . . If you would enter life, keep the commandments" (Mt 19:17). He further told him, "If you would be perfect, go, sell what you possess and give to the poor, and you will have treasure in heaven; and come, follow me" (Mt 19:21).

Jesus requested works from the man as a way to have treasure in heaven and concludes: "And every one who has left houses or brothers or sisters or father or mother or children or lands, for my name's sake, will receive a hundredfold, and inherit eternal life" (Mt 19:29).

Jesus told us clearly that a Christian must do more than call him Lord to be saved:

> "Every tree that does not bear good fruit is cut down and thrown into the fire. Thus you will know them by their fruits.

> "Not everyone who says to me, "Lord, Lord," shall enter the kingdom of heaven, but he who does the will of my Father who is in heaven" (Mt 7:19–21).
>
> "God shows no partiality, but in every nation any one who fears him and does what is right is acceptable to him" (Acts 10:35).
>
> "Let your light so shine before men, that they may see your good works and give glory to your Father who is in heaven.
>
> "Think not that I have come to abolish the law and the prophets. I have come not to abolish them but to fulfil them.... He who does [these commandments] and teaches them shall be called great in the kingdom of heaven" (Mt 5:16–19).

For those who don't do as God commands:

> Then they also will answer, "Lord, when did we see thee hungry or thirsty or a stranger or naked or sick or in prison, and did not minister to thee?" Then he will answer them, "Truly, I say to you, as you did it not to one of the least of these, you did it not to me" (Mt 25:44–45).

The Bible tells us that we can lose heaven. Our salvation does not hinge on a one-time act of being saved through faith. Once we have faith, we are firmly instructed not to veer from the course. When we stand before God for judgment, the Bible does not say we will be judged by how strong our faith is, rather, did we live out our faith to the end?

> For if we sin deliberately after receiving the knowledge of the truth, there no longer remains a sacrifice for sins . . . (Heb 10:26).
>
> Therefore do not pronounce judgment before the time . . . (1 Cor 4:5).
>
> For we share in Christ, if only we hold our first confidence firm to the end . . . (Heb 3:14).
>
> Take heed to yourself and to your teaching: hold to that,

> for by so doing you will save both yourself and your hearers (1 Tim 4:16).
>
> "But he who endures to the end will be saved" (Mt 24:13).
>
> For if, after they have escaped the defilements of the world through the knowledge of our Lord and Savior Jesus Christ, they are again entangled in them and overpowered, the last state has become worse for them than the first. For it would have been better for them never to have known the way of righteousness than after knowing it to turn back from the holy commandment delivered to them (2 Pet 2:20–21).
>
> If we endure, we shall also reign with him (2 Tim 2:12).

Even St. Paul, especially chosen by God, did not have assurance of salvation but knew he had to work to stay on track.

> I pommel my body and subdue it, lest after preaching to others I myself should be disqualified (1 Cor 9:27).
>
> But by your hard and impenitent heart, you are storing up wrath for yourself on the day of wrath when God's righteous judgment will be revealed. For he will render to every man according to his works: to those who by patience in well-doing seek for glory and honor and immortality, he will give eternal life; but for those who are factious and do not obey the truth, but obey wickedness, there will be wrath and fury (Rom 2:5–8).
>
> Therefore, my beloved, as you have always obeyed, so now, not only as in my presence but much more in my absence, work out your own salvation with fear and trembling (Phil 2:12).
>
> For we must all appear before the judgment seat of Christ, so that each one may receive good or evil, according to what he has done in the body (2 Cor 5:10).

There is no wall between faith and works. Faith is not a one-time decision, but a way of living that constantly puts demands on us to serve God and turn away from sin and from worldly things that turn us away from God. I share with my children that I have complete faith in Jesus but to follow him sometimes takes real effort. Sacrifice, giving, and doing unto others as I would have them do unto me, and resisting temptations—these are often hard choices. Think of a recovering alcoholic. He wants sobriety much like we want heaven, but attaining it is hard work on a daily basis. Because we are human, sometimes we make the wrong choices and that is where forgiveness for our sins comes in.

In the Sermon on the Mount, in Matthew's Gospel, chapter five, Jesus gives us firm instructions on how Christians are to conduct themselves. These teachings set a high standard. Accepting Jesus as your personal Lord and Savior does not naturally protect you from the pitfalls of which Jesus warns, nor does it make his instructions easy. They require struggle and choices—choices made easier through the grace of Jesus Christ, but not ones that always follow naturally with faith. Here are some of those teachings:

> "But I say to you everyone who is angry with his brother shall be liable to judgment. . . . Make friends quickly with your accuser, while you are going with him to court. . . . But I say to you that every one who looks at a woman lustfully has already committed adultery with her in his heart. . . . And if your right hand causes you to sin, cut it off and throw it away; it is better that you lose one of your members than that your whole body go into hell. . . . But I say to you, Do not resist one who is evil. But if any one strikes you on the right cheek, turn to him the other also. . . . But I say to you, Love your enemies and pray for those who persecute you, so that you may be sons of your Father who is in heaven" (Mt 5:22–45).

> "He who does not take up his cross and follow me is not worthy of me" (Mt 10:38).

In the Lord's prayer, Jesus tells us to say, "forgive us our debts as we also have forgiven our debtors" (Mt 6:12). Forgiveness is a charitable action, a good work. God demands that we forgive if we seek forgiveness from Him. Can we get into heaven without forgiveness? If we have faith in Jesus but don't forgive our grouchy neighbor, who, let's say, ran over our favorite rose-bush (on purpose, you suspect), aren't we still offending God? Or through faith, does forgiving your neighbor come easily, spontaneously? Not for me it doesn't. The above lessons from the Sermon on the Mount can be difficult choices made only with real effort, and helped by God's grace. If all we need is faith, then why pray and read the Bible, and why does the Bible give us so much instruction?

In summary of this primary topic, faith versus works, are the following excerpts from Pope John Paul's exhortation of January 22, 1999, at the Basilica of Our Lady of Guadalupe in Mexico City. He speaks of bridging faith and life:

> The greatness of the Incarnation and gratitude for the gift of the first proclamation of the Gospel in America are an invitation to respond readily to Christ with a more decisive personal conversion and a stimulus to ever more generous fidelity to the Gospel.
>
> Christ's call to conversion finds an echo in the words of the apostle: "It is time now to wake from sleep, because our salvation is closer than when we first became believers" (Rom 13: 11)
>
> The encounter with the living Jesus impels us to conversion. In this regard, St. Paul speaks of "faith working through love" (Gal 5: 6). This means that true conversion needs to be prepared and nurtured through the prayerful reading of sacred Scripture and the practice of the Sacraments of Reconciliation and the Eucharist.
>
> Conversion leads to fraternal communion because it enables us to understand that Christ is the head of the Church, his Mystical Body; it urges solidarity, because it makes us aware that whatever we do for others, especially for the poorest, we do for Christ himself. Conversion, therefore, fosters a new life, in which there is no separation between faith and works in our daily response to the universal call to holiness. . . .
>
> To be true disciples of the Lord, believers must bear witness to their faith, and "witnesses testify not only with

words, but also with their lives." We must keep in mind the words of Jesus: "Not everyone who says to me, Lord, Lord! shall enter the kingdom of heaven, but he who does the will of my Father who is in heaven" (Mt 7:21). . . .

Yet conversion is incomplete if we are not aware of the demands of the Christian life and if we do not strive to meet them. "He who does not love his brother whom he has seen, cannot love God whom he has not seen" (1 Jn 4:20)

Fraternal charity means attending to all the needs of our neighbor. "If anyone has the world's goods and sees his brother in need, yet closes his heart against him, how does God's love abide in him?" (1 Jn 3:17). . . .

It is essential to adopt a mode of living which makes us like the one who says of himself: "I am the good shepherd" (Jn 10:11), and to whom St. Paul points when he writes: "Imitate me as I imitate Christ" (1 Cor 11:1). . . .

Prayer, both personal and liturgical, is the duty of every Christian. Jesus Christ, the Good News of the Father, warns us that without him we can do nothing (Jn 15:5). He himself, in the decisive moments of his life, before doing something, used to withdraw to a quiet place to give himself to prayer and contemplation, and he asked the apostles to do the same. . . .

Christian spirituality is nourished above all by a constant sacramental life, since the sacraments are the root and endless source of God's grace, which believers need to sustain them on their earthly pilgrimage. The sacramental life needs to be complemented by the values of popular piety, values which will be enriched in turn by sacramental practice and saved from falling into the danger of routine. . . .

Conversion is directed to holiness, since conversion is not an end in itself but a journey towards God who is holy. To be holy is to be like God and to glorify his name in the works which we accomplish in our lives (see Mt 5:16)

On the path of holiness, Jesus Christ is the point of reference and the model to be imitated: He is "the Holy

> One of God," and was recognized as such (see Mk 1: 24). It is he who teaches us that the heart of holiness is love, which leads even to giving our lives for others (see Jn 15: 13). Therefore, to imitate the holiness of God, as it was made manifest in Jesus Christ his son, is nothing other than to extend in history his love, especially towards the poor, the sick and the needy, (see Lk 10: 25).
>
> "I am the Way, the Truth and the Life" (Jn 14: 6). With these words, Jesus presents himself as the path that leads to holiness. But a specific knowledge of this way comes chiefly through the Word of God which the Church proclaims in her preaching. Therefore, the Church of America must give a clear priority to prayerful reflection on sacred Scripture by all the faithful. . . .
>
> As Sacred Scripture reminds us, the old man must die and the new man must be born, that is, the whole person must be renewed "in full knowledge after the image of the Creator" (Col 3: 10).[2]

My secondary topic in this chapter—Purgatory—is a by-product of the two different beliefs on how we attain salvation. Belief or non-belief in purgatory is directly related to whether one believes we are saved by "faith alone" or not. I am including a brief discussion of it here for this reason.

Protestants believe that a person of faith goes straight to heaven because he is saved. You are either saved or not, there is no purgatory. According to them, sins are no impediment to heaven because Jesus covers our soul with his precious blood and makes it acceptable for heaven. Catholics believe we are responsible for the state of our own soul, and sin must be repented to be removed. The only time the Bible mentions covering sins refers to one man forgiving another. Between us, we can overlook sins, but only God can forgive them.

I've been to non-Catholic funerals where speakers convey their assurance that the deceased has reached heaven. "We know he is in heaven with God right now, and you can have this

---

[3] Pope John Paul II, Apostolic exhortation *Ecclesia in America*, Mexico City, January 22, 1999.

assurance too," were the words of one minister at a funeral service. Since Catholics believe that those in the state of grace but who have not made full reparation for sins are not pure enough to enter heaven, we pray for our dead—just in case. Catholics pray for the souls in purgatory to help speed their way to heaven. Since the writings on the catacombs (tombs of the very early Christians) give evidence that the dead were being prayed for by their Christian friends, we have historical confirmation for our beliefs and practices of today.

The Old Testament book of Maccabees contains reference to the Jews praying for souls after their death. We can cite the same Scripture from which Jesus read and taught to defend our practice of praying for the souls in purgatory: ". . . it was a holy and pious thought. Therefore he made atonement for the dead, that they might be delivered from their sin" (2 Mac 12:46).

Maccabees is one of the Old Testament books removed from the Protestant Bible, even though it was part of the Scripture used by Jews during the time Jesus walked the earth. The book of Maccabees has always been a part of the Bible accepted by the Catholic Church as divinely inspired.

Even without agreeing whether Maccabees belongs in the Bible or not, the book gives historical evidence that this was a practice among the Hebrew people during the second century B.C. Since some Protestants do not have the books of Maccabees in their Bible, I will use some books we share in common.

"Whoever speaks against the Holy Spirit will not be forgiven, either in this age or in the age to come" (Mt 12:32). This statement of Jesus refers to forgiveness in this age and forgiveness in the age to come. There are two different times of forgiveness given in his statement.

> May the Lord grant him to find mercy from the Lord on that Day (2 Tim 1:18). [St. Paul is praying for his departed friend, Onesiphorus.]
>
> You will never get out till you have paid the last penny (Mt 5:26).
>
> Though he himself will be saved, but only as through fire (1 Cor 3:15).

The last two passages support the existence of purgatory, a place of purification, where we are purged from our sins, where we pay our debt—every last penny.

> For Christ also died for sins once for all, the righteous for the unrighteous, that he might bring us to God, being put to death in the flesh but made alive in the spirit; in which he went and preached to the spirits in prison, who formerly did not obey, when God's patience waited in the days of Noah, during the building of the ark, in which a few, that is, eight persons, were saved through water (1 Pet 3:18–20).

> For this is why the Gospel was preached even to the dead, that though judged in the flesh like men, they might live in the spirit like God (1 Pet 4:6).

These two passages talk of disobedient spirits in prison. It cannot mean hell or heaven. Neither could it be the waiting place for righteous souls. St. Peter is writing about souls that were disobedient, but eventually saved. (The word "purgatory" is not used in Scripture, just as the words "Trinity" and "Incarnation" are not. But a third place, the prison, referred to above, has been called "purgatory"—a place for purging of our debts.)

Nothing unclean can enter heaven. Believing in Christ does not protect us from ever sinning again. Neither would "covering" our sins cleanse us of them. Covering a dirty wall with wallpaper does not clean the wall. Therefore, if we are not completely pure upon our death, we need to be cleansed of our sin: "But nothing unclean shall enter it, nor any one who practices abomination or falsehood" (Rev 21:27).

Our family often prays for the souls of departed Protestants we have known. Sometimes we were just barely acquainted with them, but we realize that it is possible they are in purgatory with no one to pray for them. It's a great way to show love for our neighbor.

13

THE UNION OF THE CHURCH OF HEAVEN AND EARTH

The faithful of the Church are in three different places: the blessed in heaven, those in purgatory, and those of us on earth. As Vatican II says:

> At the present time some of the Lord's disciples are pilgrims on earth. Others have died and are being purified, while others still are in glory, contemplating in full light, God himself triune and one, exactly as he is. All of us, however, in varying degrees and in different ways share in the same charity towards God and our neighbors, and we all sing the one hymn of glory to our God. All, indeed, . . . cleave together in Christ.[1]

"I find it easy to live the Communion of Saints of the three churches," St. Josemaría Escrivá said:

> The Church in heaven, where souls are triumphant with our Lord. The Church triumphant, because Christ was triumphant on the Cross. Then the Church being purified. Those brothers and sisters of ours who are not yet sufficiently clean and who do not wear the nuptial garment which will permit them to enter the glory of heaven. But they are safe and sure; when they are cleansed they will go to heaven and receive God's love.
>
> Finally, there is the Church Militant: you and I. There is no peace because we lack soldiers. . . . Each one of us has to be a soldier who fights with his own nature and tendencies. May you have many victories in your personal

[1] Vatican II, *Lumen Gentium*, no. 49.

> struggle each day. So, on with it! Man's life on earth is a battle. And it isn't I who say it: it's the Holy Spirit: "Man's life on earth is a battle" (Job 7: 1, Vulgate).[2]

> To know that all of us Christians form a part of the Mystical Body of Christ is a source of great joy and reassurance. The dogma of the Communion of Saints is one of the most consoling truths the Church teaches us. To know that we are intimately connected to Christ, our divine Head, and to each other; and that there is a real communication of goods among the members of the Mystical Body; and that union lasts beyond. . . .[3]

The Church has always encouraged the faithful to be familiar with the lives of the saints, to learn from them and to ask them to intercede before God on our behalf.

> They do not cease to intercede with the Father for us, as they offer the merits which they acquired on earth through the one mediator between God and men, Christ Jesus. . . . So, by their fraternal concern is our weakness greatly helped.[4]

The saints are examples of exceptional love and service to God. Through them we have heroes to emulate, examples of God's grace at work, and friends in heaven to pray for us as our friends on earth do. Praying to saints does not detract from God. It is our faith in God that leads us to call on them for help. To invoke a saint is to ask their help and intercession, knowing that all power in heaven and earth comes from God. They are no more than intercessors.

Children love to hear about the angels and saints. Why limit story time to fairy tales when there is a wealth of inspiration available in real life stories of the saints? They are members of our spiritual family; guiding our steps on this earth, inspiring us and praying for us.

Reading the lives of the saints to children is a powerful tool in giving them true examples of holiness. My children were held

---

[2] Josemaría Escrivá, *Catechesis in America.*

[3] Bishop Alvaro del Portillo, *Letter*, November 1984.

[4] *Catechism of the Catholic Church*, no. 956.

spellbound by the story of St. Isaac Jogues, a Jesuit priest captured, tortured, and made a slave by Indians. When he escaped and returned to his homeland, France, his persistent request was to return to the Indians, to instruct them, to pray for them, and, he hoped, to bring them to the happiness of the true faith. He was given permission to return, and eventually he became a martyr for his faith in Jesus Christ. Then there is St. Theresa, the Little Flower, who led a short, quiet, unspectacular life except for her burning love and devotion to God. She was hidden during life but discovered and honored after her death. One of her prayers on earth was: "I want to spend my heaven in doing good on earth." Or, as St. Dominic said to his brothers before he died: "Do not weep, for I shall be more useful to you after my death, as I shall help you there more effectively than during my life." Just as inspiring are stories of saints who did not start out holy but who converted and eventually gave all to God. It gives us hope that even though we too may be often weak and less-than-holy, we might someday become saintly. There are endless stories of heroism and always a love of God.

The usual arguments against devotion to saints are similar to those against honoring Mary, the Blessed Mother. In this chapter, I will present Scripture passages that defend the practice of invoking their aid—and also the help of the angels—through prayer. Also, I will include an explanation on the use of statues and other religious symbols as well as relics, since they can be a part of this devotion.

Usually the first argument against praying to the angels and saints is that the Bible speaks out against it: "For there is one God, and there is one mediator between God and men, the man Jesus Christ . . ." (1 Tim 2:5). Therefore, some insist, it is wrong to go to the angels and saints to ask them to pray for us.

The problem here is a lack of understanding as to what Catholics are doing when we pray to the angels and saints. Calling on them is no different from calling a devout and prayerful aunt and asking her to pray for you. You are not asking her to take Jesus' place as mediator. You just happen to know that she is a devout and prayerful person, so you would like her to pray for your intention. You would be uniting yourself in prayer with your aunt to the one mediator—Jesus Christ.

> The prayer of a righteous man has great power in its effects (Jas 5:16).

> The Lord . . . hears the prayer of the righteous (Prov 15:29).

Angels and saints are already in heaven, and certainly their prayers must be very powerful. Who can be more righteous and just than the angels and the saints, perfected and in heaven? The more prayers, and the more perfect the prayers, that are joined together with our own to God, the more our own prayers are multiplied and magnified.

The next argument against having a relationship with angels and saints is the belief that communication between earth and heaven is not possible. But Scripture tells us that we form one body with Christ our Head, that death does not separate us, and that there is ongoing communication between those on earth and those who have died.

> . . . that there may be no discord in the body, but that the members may have the same care for one another. If one member suffers, all suffer together; if one member is honored, all rejoice together (1 Cor 12:25–26).

> For as in one body we have many members, and all the members do not have the same function, so we, though many, are one body in Christ, and individually members one of another (Rom 12:4–5).

> And he came and preached peace to you who were far off and peace to those who were near; for through him we both have access in one Spirit to the Father. So then you are no longer strangers and sojourners, but you are fellow citizens with the saints and members of the household of God, built upon the foundation of the apostles and prophets, Christ Jesus himself being the cornerstone, in whom the whole structure is joined together and grows into a holy temple in the Lord; in whom you also are built into it for a dwelling place of God in the Spirit (Eph 2:17–22).

> There is one body and one Spirit, just as you were called to the one hope that belongs to your call, one Lord, one

> faith, one baptism, one God and Father of us all, who is above all and through all and in all (Eph 4:4–6).

Although most Protestants do not pray to the saints, in their creed they profess to believe in the "communion of saints." The Bible tells us that this is communication between us and those who have died.

Remember the story of Lazarus (Lk 16:19–31), the poor beggar who received no sympathy from the rich man, Dives, while on earth? After they died, Dives saw Lazarus in the bosom of Abraham and asked his intercession to cross the abyss and warn his family still on earth. Although his request was turned down, this shows the possibility of communication between those in the next world and those on earth.

During the transfiguration, Moses and Elijah appeared with Christ. They were able to appear back on earth, where they no longer lived, and converse with Jesus. "And behold, two men talked with him, Moses and Elijah, who appeared in glory and spoke of his departure, which he was to accomplish at Jerusalem" (Lk 9:30–31).

Scripture tells us that the saints see us. They are attentive to us and pray for us:

> Therefore, since we are surrounded by so great a cloud of witnesses . . . (Heb 12:1).
>
> . . . the twenty-four elders . . . each holding a harp and with golden bowls full of incense, which are the prayers of the saints (Rev 5:8).
>
> And another angel came and stood at the altar with a golden censer; and he was given much incense to mingle with the prayers of all the saints . . . (Rev 8:3.)

These passages from the book of Revelation have been interpreted to mean that the incense is made up of the petitions offered for those who need help on earth by the holy ones in heaven, the saints. Since heaven has no space or time, the angels and saints are not encumbered by the limits we live under. Rather than being able to talk to one person at one time, they can hear from everyone petitioning them at the same time—they can hear and know "fully":

> For now we see in a mirror dimly, but then face to face. Now I know in part; then I shall understand fully, even as I have been fully understood (1 Cor 13:12).

As we can hear and know much more fully in heaven than on earth, would it make sense that we would lose our ability to hear and intercede for one another as we do now? Surely our capacity for love and charity increases in heaven, not decreases? Death destroys our body, not our love and ability to intercede for one another.

Scripture reveals that the angels are aware of what we are doing. And it states that those who die and go to heaven become like the angels:

> For when they rise from the dead, they neither marry nor are given in marriage, but are like angels in heaven (Mk 12:25).

Karl Keating explains it this way:

> The ancient Jews believed in the intercession of saints. Judas Maccabaeus saw in a vision "which was worthy of belief" how two deceased men, the high priest Onias and the prophet Jeremiah, interceded with God for the Jews (2 Mac 15:11–16).
>
> And Jeremiah himself wrote that Moses and Samuel made intercession for the Jews, apparently meaning after their deaths (Jer 15:1). We learn that angels and saints place the prayers of the holy on earth at God's feet (Tob 12:12; Rev 5:8, 8:3), which is to say that they support the prayers with their intercessions, These verses have also been interpreted to mean that the angels and saints were prayed to and that they take these prayers to God.[5]

Devotion to the saints and angels often includes having pictures and statues of them. We use these as physical reminders to help us focus on them, just as we use pictures of family and friends both living and dead as reminders. Their images help us feel close to them. Pictures of saints—and also of Jesus and Mary for that matter—draw our thoughts to heaven and act as a silent witness to our faith. Is it wrong for our children to hang up pictures of favorite movie characters? Are pictures of George Washington and Abraham Lincoln sinful? Then what could be wrong with having images of those in heaven? Catholics do not think it is wrong because God himself commanded images to be made:

> And you shall make two cherubim of gold . . . on the two ends of the mercy seat. . . . The cherubim shall spread out their wings above, overshadowing the mercy seat with their wings, their faces one to another; toward the mercy seat shall the faces of the cherubim be (Ex 25:18–20).

> And the Lord said to Moses, "Make a fiery serpent, and set it on a pole; and everyone who is bitten, when he sees it, shall live" (Num 21:8).

> In the inner sanctuary he made two cherubim of olive-wood, each ten cubits high (1 Kings 6:23).

Those critical of statues and pictures used in connection with religion quote the Old Testament: "You shall not make for yourself a graven image" (Ex 20:4). Statues can be called graven images—something made by hand. Does the Bible contradict itself? No, it does not. The key to understanding this apparent contradiction is to understand what these statues were being used for. A statue used for religious purposes glorifies the Almighty. A statue that reminds us of an angel or saint is special only because the angel or saint reflects the glory and power of God. A statue used for idol worship, to represent a false god, breaks the first commandment.

Some people think statues and pictures representing Jesus are wrong and also spoken against as "graven images." Remember, during the writing of the Old Testament, the Word had not yet become flesh in the person of Jesus, God the Son. To have a man-made image of God, who was without image, who had never been seen by man, would have demeaned God. Once Jesus became man, he took on a physical appearance while he walked the earth. How could it be wrong to represent the physical person of Jesus who showed himself to us physically as the Son of God. Statues and pictures of him remind us of Jesus, and help us to be more conscious of his presence.

One last saint-related point is the veneration of holy relics. Relics are fragments of the bones of a saint or items that belonged to or were used in some way by a saint, and are now revered as special. Where do Catholics get the notion that these objects could be of any value? We get it from the Bible:

> So Elisha died, and they buried him. Now bands of Moabites used to invade the land in the spring of the year. And as a man was being buried, lo, a marauding band was seen and the man was cast into the grave of Elisha; and as soon as the man touched the bones of Elisha, he revived, and stood on his feet (2 Kings 13:20–21).
>
> A woman who had suffered from a hemorrhage for twelve years came up behind him and touched the fringe of his garment; for she said to herself, "If I only touch his garment, I shall be made well." Jesus turned, and seeing her he said, "Take heart daughter! Your faith has made you well." And instantly the woman was made well (Mt 9:20–22).
>
> So that they even carried out the sick into the streets and laid them on beds and pallets, that as Peter came by at least his shadow might fall on some of them (Acts 5:15).
>
> And God did extraordinary miracles by the hands of Paul, so that handkerchiefs or aprons were carried away from his body to the sick, and diseases left them and the evil spirits came out of them" (Acts 19:11–12).

The use and the power of relics are dependent on God. Relics are not magic or superstition. Seeking out persons who were close to Christ and things connected with them is no more out of place than was the hemorrhaging woman whose faith led her to believe that merely touching Christ's garment would be enough to heal her.

People who desire to encounter Christ closely often visit the Holy Land where he walked. The saints and the relics are things we access in our quest to be closer to God. It is no more necessary to our faith life than is a trip to Jerusalem, but both are worthy ways of bringing Jesus more fully into our lives.

If you have never acknowledged the saints, try it. Begin by buying a book for your children on the lives of the saints. Find an interesting saint and read the adult version of his or her life. See if you are not inspired and drawn closer to God through it.

Remember, the greatness of the angels and saints is only a reflection of God's own supreme greatness. So again, as the argument goes, why not go to him directly through Jesus? We do. The saints and angels are nothing more than guides or step-ladders to Jesus. These members of our Christian family in heaven can give us a boost and help us along the way.

14

FAMILY PRAYER

Although I have saved this chapter for last, prayer should be the starting point for raising and instructing our children. Bringing up Catholic children to love and serve God and to know their faith is not easy. It is hard work, but it is also God's work. Prayer acknowledges that God is in charge of all things. He offers us comfort and guidance in our life and work through prayer.

Prayer can take four forms: petition, praise, thanksgiving, and contrition. Just talking to God is a prayer and that we can do throughout the day as easily as we can think about what we'll make for dinner, or remember we had better put gas in the car. "Pray constantly" (1 Thess 5:17). By talking to God frequently and offering each day as a gift to him, we can pray without ceasing. A prayer, known as the Jesus Prayer, can easily be said throughout the day: "Lord Jesus Christ, have mercy on me." While doing ordinary activities, waiting in line or in traffic, we can meditate and repeat the words, quietly talking to Jesus.

I cannot imagine trying to raise eight children without God's constant help. At times I didn't think we could come as far as we have. Now, I can look back and see God's hand in our lives. I know it doesn't mean that we will not have problems in our family. But Mark and I believe that as long as we stay close to God and make prayer a constant in our lives, at least we will never face problems alone.

This is not the way we began our family life. Initially, we prayed only at mealtimes and bedtime with the children. Now, we start the day and end the day with prayer and typically include it in between. If I drive one of my children to work, we pray together for God's blessings and ask that he get along with his boss and co-workers and do a good job. We pray for the school day, before selling raffle tickets, to find a lost item, before any competitions, and afterward in thanksgiving, when taking a trip, and so forth.

Morning and evening prayers can become so routine that the kids only go through the motions, but some variation—perhaps a Bible or special reading, or a family novena—helps keep their attention. We have regular prayers we say together; often we say the Rosary in the evening, sometimes there is a reading, and usually the kids take turns adding their own thanks and petitions to God. We sometimes pray the stations of the cross. Mark and I try to go to daily Mass and the kids often accompany us, especially during the school year when they have to get up early anyway. We also have attended a family prayer group for more than nine years. The support and friendship of other families also seeking to put God first in their families has been invaluable.

There are still family prayer times where children have to be told to "put the toy down, leave the dog alone," or even "is anyone praying tonight?" Yet, the kids immediately turn to God on their own for all their concerns and usually remember to pray in thanksgiving for blessings. So I know even if they aren't always little saints, they are growing in their understanding that God belongs at the center of our lives.

The point is to make God a habit in your life. If you are not accustomed to praying together with your family, it might feel uncomfortable at first. The more you do it, though, the easier it gets. Even though I tell my children they all need to develop their own personal relationships with God and that means praying on their own, it is still important that we also pray with them. Our children need our example and participation.

We usually invite friends and relatives to join us for prayers during visits, but we never push it if they feel uncomfortable. While visiting friends many years ago, one of their children listened in the distance as our family said evening prayers. We overheard him ask, "Can we do that?" His dad answered, "Sure, go ahead. You can do it anytime you want." I don't know what the likelihood of this young boy praying on his own is, but I'm sure he was really asking his dad if their own family could pray together.

The younger your children are when you start, the easier it is. That does not mean it is ever too late, however. We want so much in life for our children, but there is nothing we can give them that is greater than what God can give them. If we believe this, we can and must overcome any reluctance on our own or our children's part to pray together.

Formal prayers are sometimes criticized as "vain repetition," which the Bible warns against. I agree to a point. Simply repeating a memorized prayer without putting your mind and heart into it can be vain repetition. As I tell my children, "If you aren't paying attention to your prayers, don't expect God to."

"And in praying, do not heap up empty phrases as the Gentiles do; for they think that they will be heard for their many words" (Mt 6:7).

I have heard many inspired prayers by non-Catholics. Just listen to Billy Graham for heartfelt and inspired prayer. At the same time, I have heard people babble on and on, talking almost nonsense just to keep talking/praying, long past the point of anything meaningful. The above Bible verse is not a condemnation of memorized prayer, it is warning against mindless, "vain" prayer. Right after he warned against "vain repetition," Jesus gave the apostles a specific prayer, the Lord's Prayer (the Our Father):

> "Pray then like this:
> Our Father who art in heaven,
> hallowed be thy name.
> Thy kingdom come,
> thy will be done on earth as it is in heaven.
> Give us this day our daily bread;
> and forgive us our debts,
>   as we also have forgiven our debtors;
> and lead us not into temptation,
>   but deliver us from evil."
>
> —Mt 6:9–13

Some say that Jesus was just showing us how to pray but that he never intended the Our Father to be a memorized prayer. Regardless of this opinion, it has become a memorized prayer for many denominations, including Catholics, who see beauty in repeating the words Jesus gave to us. Using a memorized or written prayer can help us to focus and meditate. Rather than thinking ahead as to what you will say next, you can concentrate on each word being prayed. And think about how often you tell your loved ones, "I love you." Does anyone tell you, "Can't you think of something more original to say?" Granted, even the words "I love you" can become "vain repetition," but it is the "vain" part that is the problem and not the repetition.

Even the angels in heaven repeat their prayers: "Day and night they never cease to sing, 'Holy, holy, holy is the Lord God almighty, who was and is and is to come" (Rev 4:8).

Prayers are powerful. The Bible mentions the need and value of prayer repeatedly:

> I appeal to you, brethren, by our Lord Jesus Christ and by the love of the Spirit, to strive together with me in your prayers to God on my behalf . . . (Rom 15:30).
>
> . . . and pray for those who persecute you (Mt 5:44)
>
> First of all, then, I urge that supplications, prayers, intercessions, and thanksgivings be made for all men . . . (1 Tim 2:1).
>
> So Peter was kept in prison; but earnest prayer for him was made to God by the church (Acts 12:5).
>
> And I tell you, Ask, and it will be given you; seek, and you will find; knock, and it will be opened to you. For every one who asks receives; and he who seeks finds; and to him who knocks it will be opened. What father among you, if his son asks for a fish, will instead of a fish will give him a serpent; or if he asks for an egg, will give him a scorpion? If you then, who are evil, know how to give good gifts to your children, how much more will the heavenly Father give the Holy Spirit to those who ask him! (Lk 11:9–11).

The Bible tells us to be persistent in our prayers. God sees everything, and we only see the here and now. Therefore, what we are asking for may not be in our best interest in an eternal sense. Or perhaps, we will have to wait for our answer.

> . . . because of his importunity he will rise and give him whatever he needs (Lk 11:8).

> And he told them a parable, to the effect that they ought always to pray and not lose heart. . . . Will not God vindicate his elect, who cry to him day and night? (Lk 18: 1, 7).

* * *

The following are some traditional Catholic prayers:

The Sign of the Cross

In the name of the Father, and of the Son, and of the Holy Spirit. Amen.

The Our Father

Our Father who art in heaven, hallowed be thy name. Thy kingdom come, thy will be done on earth as it is in heaven. Give us this day our daily bread; and forgive us our trespasses as we forgive those who trespass against us. And lead us not into temptation, but deliver us from evil. Amen.

The Hail Mary

Hail, Mary, full of grace, the Lord is with you. Blessed are you among women and blessed is the fruit of your womb, Jesus. Holy Mary, mother of God, pray for us sinners, now and at the hour of our death. Amen.

Glory Be

Glory be to the Father, and to the Son, and to the Holy Spirit.
As it was in the beginning, is now, and ever shall be, world without end . Amen.

Morning Prayers

Heavenly Father I give you today,
a gift of all my work and my play.
Teach me, guide me, keep me good,
help me do the things I should.

In the name of our Lord Jesus Christ I will begin this day. I thank you, Lord, for having preserved me during the night. I will do my best to make all I do today pleasing to you and in accordance with your will. My mother Mary, watch over me this day. My guardian angel, take care of me. St. Joseph and all you saints of God, pray for me.

Daily Offering

O Jesus, through the Immaculate Heart of Mary, I offer you my prayers, works, joys and sufferings of this day in union with the holy sacrifice of the Mass throughout the world. I offer them for all the intentions of your Sacred Heart: the salvation of souls, reparation for sin, and the reunion of all Christians. I offer them for the intentions of our bishops and of all the apostles of prayer, and in particular for those recommended by our Holy Father this month.

Act of Contrition

O my God, I am sorry for my sins; in choosing to sin and failing to do good. I have sinned against you and your Church. I firmly intend with the help of your Son to make up for my sins and to love as I should.

(or)

O my God, I am heartily sorry for having offended you, and I detest all my sins because I dread the loss of heaven and the pains of hell, but most of all because they offend you, my God, who are all good and deserving of all my love. I firmly resolve, with the help of your grace, to confess my sins, to do penance and to amend my life.

(or)

O my God, I am heartily sorry for having offended you. And I confess all my sins because of your just punishments. But most of all, because I have offended you my God, who art all good and deserving of all my love. I firmly resolve with the help of your grace to sin no more and avoid the near occasions of sin.

Prayers before and after Meals

Bless us O Lord, and these thy gifts, which we are about to receive from thy bounty, through Christ our Lord. Amen.

We give you thanks, almighty God, for these and all your benefits, which we have received from your bounty, through Christ our Lord. Amen.

Anima Christi

Soul of Christ, make me holy. Body of Christ, save me. Blood of Christ, fill me with love. Water from Christ's side, wash me. Passion of Christ, strengthen me. Good Jesus, hear me. Within your wounds, hide me. Never let me be parted from you. From the evil enemy, protect me. At the hour of my death, call me, and tell me to come to you, that with your saints I may praise you through all eternity. Amen.

Prayer to One's Guardian Angel

Angel of God, my guardian dear, to whom God's love commits me here, ever this day, be at my side, to light and guard, to rule and guide. Amen.

The Memorare

Remember, O most loving Virgin Mary, that never was it known that anyone who fled to your protection, implored your help, or sought your intercession was left unaided. Inspired by this confidence, we turn to you, O Virgin of Virgins, our Mother. To you we come, before you we stand, sinful and sorrowful. O Mother of the Word Incarnate, do not despise our petitions, but in your mercy hear and answer us.

Prayer to the Holy Spirit

Breathe into me Holy Spirit, that all my thoughts may be holy. Move in me, Holy Spirit, that my work, too, may be holy. Attract my heart, Holy Spirit, that I may love only what is holy. Strengthen me, Holy Spirit, that I may defend all that is holy. Protect me, Holy Spirit, that I always may be holy.

Fatima Rosary Prayer *

O my Jesus, forgive us our sins, and save us from the fires of hell. Lead all souls to heaven, especially those most in need of your mercy.

---

* Often said at the end of each decade of the rosary.

The Angelus

The angel of the Lord declared unto Mary:
And she conceived of the Holy Spirit.
Hail Mary, full of grace . . .
Behold the handmaid of the Lord:
Be it done unto me according to thy word.
Hail Mary, full of grace . . .
And the Word was made Flesh.
And dwelt among us.
Hail Mary, full of grace . . .
Pray for us, O holy Mother of God:
That we may be made worthy of the promises of Christ.

Let us pray: Pour forth, we beseech you, O Lord, your grace into our hearts; that we, to whom the Incarnation of Christ your Son was made known by the message of an Angel, may, by his passion and cross, be brought to the glory of his resurrection, through the same Christ our Lord. Amen.

The Apostles' Creed

I believe in God, the Father Almighty, Creator of heaven and earth; and in Jesus Christ, his only Son, our Lord: who was conceived by the Holy Spirit, born of the Virgin Mary, suffered under Pontius Pilate, was crucified, died and was buried. He descended to the dead; the third day he rose again from the dead; he ascended into heaven, and is seated at the right hand of God the Father Almighty; from thence he shall come to judge the living and the dead. I believe in the Holy Spirit, the holy catholic Church, the communion of saints, the forgiveness of sins, the resurrection of the body, and life everlasting. Amen.

Prayer for Vocations

Lord Jesus Christ, Shepherd of souls, who called the apostles to be fishers of men, raise up new apostles in your holy Church. Teach them that to serve you is to reign: to possess you is to possess all things. Kindle in the young hearts of our people the fire of zeal for souls. Make them eager to spread your Kingdom upon earth. Grant them courage to follow you, who are the Way, the Truth and the Life; who lives and reigns for ever and ever. Amen.

(or)

Jesus, High Priest and Redeemer forever, we beg you to call young men and women to your service as priests and religious. May they be inspired by the lives of dedicated priests, brothers, and sisters. Give to parents the grace of generosity and trust toward you and their children so that their sons and daughters may be helped to choose their vocations in life with wisdom and freedom.

The Angel's Prayer at Fatima

Most Holy Trinity, Father, Son, and Holy Spirit, I adore you profoundly. I offer you the most precious Body, Blood, Soul and Divinity of Jesus Christ, present in all the tabernacles of the world, in reparation for the outrages, sacrileges and indifference by which he is offended. And through the infinite merits of his Most Sacred Heart, and the Immaculate Heart of Mary, I beg of you the conversion of poor sinners.

The Rosary

The rosary consists of four sets of five mysteries with twenty decades of prayers. Although technically a full rosary is all twenty decades, usually, when saying a rosary, particularly in a group, only one set of the mysteries (five decades) is said. In 2002, in his Apostolic Letter on the Rosary, Pope John Paul II added the five Luminous mysteries to the traditional Joyful, Sorrowful, and Glorious mysteries. The purpose of the new mysteries was to help the Rosary "to become more fully a 'compendium of the Gospel,' by adding mysteries connected with the public life of Jesus."

How to Say the Rosary

In the name of the Father, and of the Son, and of the Holy Spirit. Amen.

Apostles Creed
Our Father
Three Hail Marys
Glory Be

(Before each decade, announce the mystery; and meditate on it as you say the Our Father, ten Hail Marys, and the Glory Be.)

(If one wishes, each decade can be followed by the Fatima Rosary prayer: "O my Jesus, forgive us our sins, save us from the fires of hell. Lead all souls to heaven, especially those most in need of thy mercy.")

The Joyful Mysteries

1. Annunciation of Our Lord
   (The angel Gabriel comes to announce to Mary that she has been chosen to be the mother of Jesus.)
2. The Visitation
   (Mary visits her cousin Elizabeth and stays with her for three months before the birth of John the Baptist.)
3. The Nativity of Jesus
   (While Mary and Joseph were in Bethlehem, she gave birth to Jesus and laid him in a manger.)
4. The Presentation in the Temple
   (Mary and Joseph brought Jesus to Jerusalem so that he could be presented to God the Father, when the day of purification came, according to the law of Moses.)
5. The Finding in the Temple
   (For three days Mary and Joseph searched for the child Jesus and then found him teaching in the midst of the teachers in the temple.)

The Luminous Mysteries

1. The Baptism in the Jordan
   (Jesus is baptized by John the Baptist, and a voice from heaven proclaims him as God's Son.)
2. The Wedding Feast of Cana
   (At the request of his mother, Jesus performs his first miracle, changing water into wine.)
3. Christ's proclamation of the Kingdom of God, with his call to conversion,
   (Various scenes from Christ's public life can be considered here.)
4. The Transfiguration
   (Christ appears in glory before three of his apostles.)
5. The Last Supper
   (Christ's institution of the Eucharist as the sacramental expression of the Paschal Mystery.)

The Sorrowful Mysteries

1. The Agony in the Garden
   (After the Last Supper, before his arrest, Jesus went to the garden of Gethsemane to pray.)
2. The Scourging at the Pillar
   (After his arrest, Jesus is scourged [whipped and beaten] at the pillar.)
3. The Crowning with Thorns
   (A crown of thorns was fixed on Christ's head as he was mocked by the soldiers.)
4. The Carrying of the Cross
   (Jesus carried the heavy cross on which he was to be crucified.)
5. The Crucifixion and Death
   (After hanging on the cross for three hours, Jesus uttered a loud cry, "Father, into your hands I commend my spirit." Then he died.)

The Glorious Mysteries

1. The Resurrection of Our Lord
   (On the third day, Jesus rose from the dead as he had promised.)
2. The Ascension into Heaven
   (Forty days after his resurrection, Jesus ascended into heaven but promised to send the Holy Spirit.)
3. The Descent of the Holy Spirit
   (The Holy Spirit descended on the apostles and the Blessed Mother in the form of tongues of fire.)
4. The Assumption of Mary
   (Mary is assumed, body and soul into heaven, reunited with her Divine Son.)
5. The Coronation of Mary.
   (Mary was crowned Queen of Heaven. "A great portent appeared in heaven, a woman clothed with the sun, with the moon under her feet, and on her head a crown of twelve stars" [Rev 12:1].)

Hail Holy Queen

Hail Holy Queen, Mother of Mercy, our life, our sweetness and our hope. To you do we cry, poor banished children of Eve. To you do we send up our sighs, mourning and weeping in this valley of tears. Turn then, most gracious advocate, thine eyes of mercy toward us, and after this our exile show unto us the blessed fruit of your womb, Jesus.

O clement, O loving, O sweet Virgin Mary.

Pray for us, O holy Mother of God, that we may be made worthy of the promises of Christ.

Prayer after the Rosary

O God, whose only-begotten Son, by his life, death, and resurrection, has purchased for us the rewards of eternal life, grant, we beseech Thee, that by meditating upon these Mysteries of the most holy rosary of the Blessed Virgin Mary, we may imitate what they contain and obtain what they promise, through Christ our Lord. Amen.

The Litany of Our Lady

Lord, have mercy on us.
Christ have mercy on us.
Lord, have mercy on us. Christ, hear us.
Christ, graciously hear us.
God the Father of heaven, *Have mercy on us.*
God the Son, Redeemer of the world,
God the Holy Spirit,
Holy Trinity, one God,
Holy Mary, *Pray for us.*
Holy Mother of God,
Holy Virgin of virgins,
Mother of Christ,
Mother of the Church,
Mother of divine grace,
Mother most pure,
Mother most chaste,
Mother inviolate,
Mother undefiled,
Mother most amiable,
Mother most admirable,
Mother of good counsel,
Mother of our Creator,

Mother of our Savior,
Virgin most prudent,
Virgin most venerable,
Virgin most renowned,
Virgin most powerful,
Virgin most merciful,
Virgin most faithful,
Mirror of justice,
Seat of wisdom,
Cause of our joy,
Spiritual vessel,
Vessel of honor,
Singular vessel of devotion,
Mystical rose,
Tower of David,
Tower of ivory,
House of gold,
Ark of the covenant,
Gate of heaven,
Morning star,
Health of the sick,
Refuge of sinners,
Comforter of the afflicted,
Help of Christians,
Queen of angels,
Queen of patriarchs,
Queen of prophets,
Queen of apostles,
Queen of martyrs,
Queen of confessors,
Queen of virgins,
Queen of all saints,
Queen conceived without original sin,
Queen assumed into heaven,
Queen of the most holy Rosary,
Queen of the family,
Queen of peace,
℣. Lamb of God, who takes away the sins of the world,
℟. Spare us, O Lord.

℣. Lamb of God, who takes away the sins of the world,
℟. Graciously hear us, O Lord.
℣. Lamb of God, who takes away the sins of the world,
℟. Have mercy on us.
Let us pray:

O God, whose only-begotten Son, by his life, death, and resurrection, has purchased for us the rewards of everlasting life; grant, we beseech you, that, we, who meditate on these mysteries of the most holy Rosary of the Blessed Virgin Mary, may imitate what they contain, and obtain what they promise.

Through Christ our Lord.
Amen.

The Stations of the Cross

The Stations of the Cross is a Catholic devotion whereby we pray and meditate on Jesus' suffering at his crucifixion. There have been many different meditations, hymns, and prayers written for each station. I will condense here the meditations from *The Way of the Cross for Children*, by Rev. Jude Winkler, O.F.M. Conv. (Catholic Book Publishing Co., New York: 1993).

℣. We adore you, O Christ, and we bless you.
℟. Because by your holy Cross you have redeemed the world.

1. *Jesus is Condemned to Death*
The leaders of the people brought Jesus before Pilate, the Roman governor. He wanted to set Jesus free, but the people demanded that Jesus be put to death. Pilate washed his hands to show he was not guilty of the blood of Jesus, and then he sent him out to be nailed to the Cross.

2. *Jesus Takes Up His Cross*
The soldiers treated Jesus with great cruelty. They beat him and placed a crown of thorns on his head. Then they led him outside and placed the wood of the Cross on his shoulder. They made him carry the Cross as they led him to the place where he would die.

3. *Jesus Falls the First Time*
Jesus had not been allowed to sleep all night, and he was now exhausted. He had been beaten and whipped, and he was near-

ing the end of his strength. Even as he tried to walk along, the soldiers continued to push and shove him. Finally, it was too much for him, and he fell down.

4. *Jesus Meets his Mother, Mary*
As the soldiers dragged Jesus through the streets, they led him to the place where Mary, his Mother, was standing. Mary felt such great sorrow to see her only Son suffering such horrible pain. Yet Jesus had assured her that he must fulfill the Father's will. So she surrendered her Son to the will of the Father.

5. *Simon Helps Jesus Carry the Cross*
The soldiers realized that Jesus was too weak to carry his Cross all the way to Calvary. They began to worry that he might die along the way. So they forced a man who was standing nearby, Simon of Cyrene, to carry the Cross for Jesus the rest of the way.

6. *Veronica Wipes the Face of Jesus*
Jesus was now totally exhausted. Many of the people around him mocked him and spit at Him. One courageous woman, named Veronica, came forward and wiped the face of Jesus with her veil. God rewarded her loving kindness, for he caused an image of the face of Jesus to appear on her veil.

7. *Jesus Falls the Second Time*
The soldiers kept leading Jesus along, but he continued to grow weaker and weaker. Once again, his strength failed him and he fell to the ground. The soldiers immediately forced him to get back on his feet and to continue his cruel journey.

8. *Jesus Meets the Weeping Women*
As Jesus struggled along, he encountered a group of women who were weeping for him. He looked up and told them that they should not weep for him, but rather for themselves and their children.

9. *Jesus Falls the Third Time*
Jesus' strength now failed him completely. He was near the place where he was to be crucified, but he could not go another step. He fell to the ground, ready to die there. But once again the soldiers forced him up, and Jesus somehow found the strength to finish his terrible journey.

10. *Jesus Is Stripped of his Clothes*
When they reached the place where Jesus was to die, the soldiers ripped off the robe that Jesus had been wearing. They were going to cut it up into pieces to divide among themselves. But when they saw it was made from one piece of cloth, they decided to roll dice for it.

11. *Jesus Is Nailed to the Cross*
The soldiers then threw Jesus to the ground and began to nail him to the Cross. They used one nail for each of his hands and one for both of his feet. Jesus felt horrible pain as they were driving the nails into his flesh.

12. *Jesus Dies on the Cross*
Jesus was crucified at noon, and he hung on the Cross for about three hours. Even then, he did not forget his love for us. When the end was near, he looked up into the heavens and said, "Father, forgive them, for they do not know what they are doing." Then he gave his spirit over to the Father and breathed his last.

13. *Jesus Is Taken Down from the Cross*
As evening approached, some of the disciples went and asked Pilate for permission to take down the body of Jesus. They lowered him to the ground and placed him in the arms of Mary, his loving Mother.

14. *Jesus is Placed in the Tomb*
It was now important to bury the body of Jesus quickly, for it was almost sunset. They brought the body to a nearby garden where there was a new tomb that belonged to Joseph of Arimathea, who was also a disciple. They laid our Lord's body in the tomb and covered the entrance to the tomb with a rock.

(Sometimes added, but usually not during Lent)

15. *Jesus Rises from the Dead*
Early on Sunday morning some of the women went to the tomb where Jesus had been buried. They found that the stone had been rolled back. An angel told them that Jesus had risen from the grave. The women told the other disciples the good news. Jesus then appeared to them and said to them, "Peace be with you."

Conclusion
Love, then, consists in this: not that we have loved God but that he has loved us and has sent his Son as an offering for our sins. Beloved, if God has loved us so, we must have the same love for one another.

Chaplet of Divine Mercy

(Recited on rosary beads)
Our Father
Hail Mary
Apostles' Creed
(On the Our Father beads)
Eternal Father, I offer You the Body and Blood, Soul and divinity of Your dearly beloved Son, Our Lord Jesus Christ, in atonement for our sins and those of the whole world.
(On the Hail Mary beads)
For the sake of his sorrowful Passion, have mercy on us and on the whole world.
(In conclusion, recited three times)
Holy God, Holy Mighty One, Holy Immortal One, have mercy on us and on the whole world.

* * *

Through prayer, we grow in our relationship with Christ. If you don't make time for prayer, you are not making time for God. Just as nothing can replace exercise to keep our bodies in shape, so nothing can replace prayer to keep our souls in shape. It is a fitting analogy for me because I make an effort to get regular exercise and know all too well how quickly a body can get out of shape without it. Just as we lose ground if we take time off from exercising, neglecting prayer causes us to slip spiritually.

Don't feel overwhelmed if you have not included much prayer in your family up until now. And do not compare your family with others. Just keep praying and asking God to take you to the next step. Increase your own efforts and trust in God to make up for what might seem beyond you. There are families I look up to as doing better than ours on many fronts. But I know we did not get where we are overnight, so even if we just take baby steps toward Jesus, they add up. That doesn't mean we don't slip, and sometimes it feels like we take a few steps backwards. Nevertheless, if we pick ourselves up and begin the journey again, perhaps even our backsliding will be a lesson and in some way still be a step forward.

I will end this chapter and this book by sharing some additional personal experiences to show you how prayer has worked for us. Ever since putting God in the driver's seat of our lives, we have relied on prayer for his guidance. What a striking "before and after" difference since we have made this change! Prayer has guided us through big decisions like buying and selling houses and having more children, as well as the smaller ones like saving a wayward duck and finding misplaced items.

Our reliance on prayer really began after Mark was laid off from a job.

I was pregnant with our fourth child, and people often tried to comfort me saying, "Don't worry, everything will turn out okay." But I realized no one could guarantee us anything. I began replying, "It might not, you know. It could be that God wants us to struggle, if that is what's best for us spiritually."

Jesus told us repeatedly that following him does not guarantee a "happily-ever-after" in this world but only in the next. We will all have struggles and crosses to bear. "He who does not take his cross and follow me is not worthy of me" (Mt 10:38).

Mark and I prayed to find a secure job for him in a community that would be good both for raising a family and growing spiritually. We put our lives in God's hands and trusted his will would be done. Every time Mark was turned down, we felt that that job wasn't God's will for us.

A month before Mark's unemployment benefits were to run out, he received a call from Bismarck, North Dakota. A radio station there was looking for a radio news broadcaster, and Mark had been recommended. My heart sank. Bismarck, North Dakota, of all places! Living in Montana for six years, we had heard endless North Dakota jokes. The land of the Great Plains and frigid winters was not my idea of a fun place to live. Mark followed up with a résumé and work samples. Within weeks we had packed and moved to Bismarck. And guess what? We've been here for twelve years, and we love it! We often laugh that it was a good thing God was calling the shots and not us.

Sometimes our prayers seem to go unanswered for long periods, and sometimes we get different answers than we asked for, making it necessary to persevere in prayer and accept with faith and hope what is not our choosing. Regardless, God's hand in our lives has become clear to us. We do sometimes grow impatient and wish for faster or different answers, but we never doubt. With every request we make, we always add, "If it is your will."

Of course, God's will is not always easy to accept. Friends from our prayer group have helped us by their example in accepting that prayers do not always receive a "yes."

Our friends Ben and Diane Roller lost their little girl, Betsy, to cancer several years ago. They prayed endlessly and begged God to heal her. He did not. Toward the end of Betsy's illness her parents helped her prepare to say good-bye and to meet God. It was bittersweet when Betsy explained she would be happy whatever happened because, "either I'll be here with you and my brothers or I'll be in heaven with Jesus."

A couple of years after Betsy's death, Diane told me that if she could wish her daughter back she would not. Although not a day went by that she did not miss Betsy, Diane said she knew Betsy was happier in heaven with Jesus than she had been on earth. She also said that the thought of her own death no longer frightened her because then she will see her daughter again. Diane and Ben credit their faith in God and their prayers with strengthening them enough to accept and work through the grief and still embrace each day.

Mark and I have confronted the mortality of our children firsthand, and we instinctively did it with prayer and faith. While at a family reunion one summer, my son Aaron, fifteen at the time, cried out in alarm that there was something wrong with Tyler, then age ten. Mark and I found him not breathing and turning blue. Mark ran to get his brother, Scott, a doctor. In a panic, another son, Luke, and I attempted CPR, not realizing there actually was still a pulse.

While awaiting help, everyone instinctively prayed for God's help. Yet, even then, I prayed for God's will to be done. I did not know if Tyler was even still alive. I told God, "He's in your hands," begging to have him back, but thinking that he might already be with God. Later, Mark told me he did the same, all the while wondering if he would ever be with Tyler again until they both reached heaven.

It turned out to be a seizure from which Tyler fully recovered, and he has not experienced one since. The next morning, Mark and I talked about the ordeal as a family. Tyler, too, temporarily conscious when struggling to breathe, thought death had come for him. I told the kids what had happened was actually a blessing from God. We will all die one day, and we were given a glimpse of how unexpectedly death can come. God had helped us to appreciate Tyler's presence with us, because we thought we had lost him. We realized that we might not have a chance to say good-bye to our loved ones, and that we should live each day serving God and each other because there aren't always second chances.

The thought of losing what is most precious to us, our children, touches the heart of every parent. Our children are our greatest gift and greatest responsibility. As frightening as the thought of losing them physically is, it is even scarier to think of not being reunited as a family in heaven someday. Surely, our foremost task in life is to teach our children to love and serve God. We cannot insure that they become saints, but we must fulfill our God-given responsibility and do our best to instruct them according to God's will.

Even though I have written a whole book on the topic, I suppose I will always feel there are areas where I could do better. I would never want to be held up as an example of "the perfect Catholic family" because we definitely are not. If we are to be an example at all, it should be that of a family that still stumbles forward but has come a long way through the grace of God and, thankfully, we continue to press on.

I have shared my story and some of the answers I have found over the years with you because I believe this is a journey we are on together. When we pray for our families we should pray for all families everywhere, struggling to do the job God wants of us. Let us pray for each other that we will be the parents God wants us to be and that, with his grace, we will adequately pass on Catholic truths to our children.

Bibliography

Akin, James, "Infant Baptism," *This Rock*, vol. 8, no. 5 (May 1997).

Alexander, Anthony F., *College Apologetics: Proof of the Truth of the Catholic Faith* (Chicago: Henry Regnery Co., 1954; repr. Rockford, Ill.: Tan Books, 1994).

Angelica, Mother M., *Mother Angelica's Answers, Not Promises* (New York: Harper & Row, 1987; repr. San Francisco: Ignatius Press, 1996).

Burnham, Jim, and Frank Chacon, *Beginning Apologetics I* (Farmington, N.M.: San Juan Catholic Seminars, 1993).

Bruskewitz, Fabian W., *The Little Catechism on Confession* (Lincoln, Neb.: 1996).

Budnik, Mary Ann, *Looking for Peace? Try Confession* (Springfield, Ill.: R. B. Media, Inc., 1997).

Carroll, Anne W., *Christ the King: Lord of History* (Rockford, Ill.: Tan Books, 1976).

Catechism of the Catholic Church (various publishers, 1994).

Chervin, Ronda, *Signs of Love* (Boston: St. Paul Books, 1992).

Clowes, Brian, *Call to Action or Call to Apostasy?* (Front Royal, Va.: Human Life International, 1997).

Currie, David B., *Born Fundamentalist, Born Again Catholic* (San Francisco: Ignatius Press, 1996).

Early Christian Writings (Penquin Books, 1968, 1987).

Filippo, Stephen N., "Sacred Scripture Depends on Sacred Tradition," *This Rock*, vol. 11, no. 3 (March 2000).

Fox, Robert J., *Covenant with Jesus* (New Hope, Ky.: St. Martin de Porres Community, Fatima Family Apostolate, 1996).

———, *Fundamentals of Faith* (New Hope, Ky.: St. Martin de Porres Community, Fatima Family Apostolate, 1997).

———, *Only Heroic Catholic Families Will Survive* (New Hope, Ky.: St. Martin de Porres Community, Fatima Family Apostolate, 1994).

Ghezzi, Bert, "Keeping Your Kids Catholic Workshop" [audio tapes] (Huntington, Ind.: Our Sunday Visitor).

Gibbons, Cardinal James, *The Faith of Our Fathers* (1876; repr. Rockford, Ill.: Tan Books, 1980).

Glenn, Paul J., *Apologetics: A Philosophic Defense and Explanation of the Catholic Religion* (Herder Book Co., 1931; repr. Rockford, Ill.: Tan Books, 1980).

Graham, Henry G., *Where We Got the Bible: Our Debt to the Catholic Church* (Rockford Ill.: Tan Books, 1987).

Hahn, Scott, "How to Get the Most out of Mass" [audio tapes] (West Covina, Calif.: Saint Joseph Communications).

Hunt, Duane G., "Why I Defend the Church," *This Rock*, vol. 9, no. 4 (April 1998).

Jindal, Boby, "How Catholicism Is Different", *New Oxford Review*, vol. 63, no. 10 (December 1996).

Jones, Alex, "Return to Apostolic Traditions," *This Rock*, vol. 11, nos. 7–8 (July–August 2000).

Keating, Karl, *Catholicism and Fundamentalism* (San Francisco: Ignatius Press, 1988).

Keating Karl, *The Usual Suspects* (San Francisco: Ignatius Press, 2000).

———, *What Catholics Really Believe—Setting the Record Straight: 52 Answers to Common Misconceptions about the Catholic Faith* (Ann Arbor, Mich.: Servant Publications, 1992).

Kelley, Bennet, C.P., *The New Saint Joseph Baltimore Catechism*, No. 1 (New York: Catholic Book Publishing Co., 1964).

Kreeft, Peter, et al., *Talking to Your Children about Being Catholic* (Huntington, Ind.: Our Sunday Visitor, 1995).

Lovasik, Lawrence, *The Holy Eucharist* (New York: Catholic Book Publishing Co., 1986).

Madrid, Patrick, *Surprised by Truth* (San Diego: Basilica Press, 1994).

Nevins, Albert J., M.M., *Scriptures of Faith: Cornerstone of Catholicism* (Huntington, Ind.: Our Sunday Visitor, 1992).

O'Reilly, Steven, "The One Who Serves," *This Rock*, vol. 11, nos. 7–8 (July–August 2000).

Pavlat, Eric K., "Teenaged Protestants Study Mary," *This Rock*, vol. 9, no. 5 (May 1998).

Pillar of Fire, Pillar of Truth (San Diego: Catholic Answers, 1996).

Roberts, Kenneth J., *Proud to Be Catholic* (Huntington, Ind.: Our Sunday Visitor, 1995).

Rumble and Carty, *Radio Replies* (Rockford, Ill.: Tan Books, 1979).

Schreck, Alan, *The Compact History of the Catholic Church* (Ann Arbor, Mich.: Servant Books, 1987).

Shea, Mark, "When His Body Met My Soul," *Our Sunday Visitor*, vol. 87, no. 49 (April 4, 1999).

Stenson, James B., *Anchor: God's Promises of Hope to Parents* (New York: Scepter, 2003).

———, *Compass: A Handbook on Parent Leadership* (New York: Scepter, 2003).

———, *Father: The Family Protector* (New York: Scepter, 2004).

Stravinskas, Peter M. J., *The Mass: A Biblical Prayer* (Huntington, Ind.: Our Sunday Visitor, 1987, 1989).

Whitcomb, Paul, *Confession of a Roman Catholic* (repr. Rockford, Ill.: Tan Books, 1985).

Winkler, Jude, O.F.M. Conv., *The Way of the Cross for Children* (New York: Catholic Book Publishing Co., 1993).

Some other useful books for parents are:

Abad, Javier, and Eugenio Fenoy, *Marriage a Path to Sanctity* (Manila: Sinag-Tala Publishers, 1988).

Bonacci, Mary Beth, *Real Love* (San Francisco: Ignatius Press).

Bonacci, Mary Beth, *We're on a Mission from God* (San Francisco: Ignatius Press, 1996).

Budnik, Mary Ann, *Raising Happier Children through a Happier Marriage* (Springfield, Ill.: R. B. Media, Inc.).

Burke, Cormac, *Covenanted Happiness* (New York: Scepter Publishers, 2001).

Campbell, Ross, *How to Really Love your Child* (Colorado Springs: Chariot Victor).

Escrivá, Josemaría, "Marriage a Christian Vocation," in *Christ Is Passing By* (New York: Scepter, 1974).

Guarendi, Ray, *Raising Kids Right: Giving Parenting Back to Parents* [audio tapes] (San Diego: Catholic Answers).

Isaacs, David, *Character Building: A Guide for Parents and Teachers* (New York: Scepter, 1994).

Stenson, James B., *Lifeline: The Religious Upbringing of Your Children* (New York: Scepter, 1996).

Welborn, Amy, *Prove It! God; Prove It! Jesus; Prove It! Church; Prove It! Prayer* [four books] (Huntington, Ind.: Our Sunday Visitor, 1999–2003).